ERRATA

The text on page 68 should be read after the second paragraph under the heading "Transition curves" on page 66, i.e. – after the words "The transition curve is established as follows:—"

The cover picture shows a scene during a Locomotive Rally at the track of the West Riding Small Locomotive Society, and was reproduced from a colour photograph by Mr. J. A. Hartup of Lancaster.

OUTDOOR MODEL RAILWAYS

Outdoor

Model Railways

by
MARTIN EVANS
Editor of
MODEL ENGINEER

MODEL & ALLIED PUBLICATIONS LTD.
13/35 Bridge Street, Hemel Hempstead, Herts
1970

Also by Martin Evans
MANUAL OF
MODEL STEAM LOCOMOTIVE CONSTRUCTION
MODEL LOCOMOTIVE BOILERS
MODEL LOCOMOTIVE VALVE GEARS

Locomotive History
ATLANTIC ERA
PACIFIC STEAM
FROM INVERNESS TO CREWE

Trade Distributors:

ARGUS PRESS LTD., 12-18 Paul Street, London, EC2A 4JS

Printed by

Gilmour & Dean Ltd. Hamilton and London

Contents

List of Drawings

Introduction

DURING THE LAST FIFTEEN years or so, the popularity of the "live steam" locomotive seems to have increased enormously, so it is not surprising that a good many books have been published on this subject. Yet, as far as I am aware, not a single work has appeared dealing with the construction of the track or lineside accessories.

A rather similar situation seems also to exist as regards the smaller gauges of model railway, for several books have been published dealing with the locomotives and rolling stock, though these have been mainly concerned with the typical indoor electrically-driven line.

As far as the Gauge "O" and "I" railways are concerned, with the small size of the average modern house, the garden seems to be the obvious place for their layout and operation, and in the first part of this book, I have endeavoured to give some general hints and tips which I hope will be found of some assistance to the less experienced model railwayman.

The second part deals with the larger gauge railways, for the hauling of passengers on gauges from $2\frac{1}{2}$ in. to 15 in. It seems astonishing that nothing has been written about how to lay a garden track, whether of the raised or ground-level variety, for the very popular $3\frac{1}{2}$ in., 5 in. and $7\frac{1}{4}$ in. gauge steam locomotive, apart from short articles which have appeared from time to time in the magazine *Model Engineer*.

To deal with the enormous variety of subjects that go to make up the miniature outdoor railway in all its ramifications in one single volume, has meant that each has been covered rather sketchily. For instance, it would be quite possible to fill one book of this size on the single subject of track-laying, or of signalling. Nevertheless, I hope and believe that the work will prove useful, especially to beginners in this fascinating hobby, or to those with limited experience who wish to lay out a garden railway, or to those Officials of the smaller clubs and societies who may not be fortunate enough to number civil engineers, surveyors or architects among their members.

Finally, I would like to record my grateful thanks to Lord Gretton of Stapleford Park, for great assistance with photographs, to Mr. D. E. Lawrence of the Bournemouth Society, for much help and advice, and to Mr. Cyril E. Smith of the Coventry Society, for contributing the final chapter.

Hemel Hempstead, 1969.   MARTIN EVANS.

CHAPTER ONE

Sites and Scales

WITH THE SMALL SIZE of the modern house, particularly in Great Britain, many model railway enthusiasts are thinking about using their gardens as sites for their railway. Even in pre-war days, very few of us could spare a really large room in the house exclusively for the model railway; even if a room was acquired, this seldom led to good domestic relations.

Indoor lines for gauge "o" and gauge "1" usually have to be accommodated in an attic or roof-space or in a cellar. On the whole a cellar is much to be preferred to an attic because although a cellar is sometimes troubled with dampness, it will not be stifling hot in mid-summer or perishing cold in the winter.

The enthusiast will, therefore, appreciate that the arguments for taking the model railway out into the garden are very good ones. Agreed that the garden railway cannot be used when it is raining or on cold winter nights, yet there are many days during the British winter when conditions for operating the garden railway are ideal. Even a severe frost can be overcome.

The space problem is nothing like so acute if even only a small garden is available. Of course, if the owner of the model railway is a gardening enthusiast, he may not be so keen on digging holes for the various supporting posts or building miniature embankments and viaducts amongst the flowers. Yet a model garden railway in gauge "o" or "1" can be blended in with the rural surroundings of the garden so skilfully that even the enthusiastic gardener is not offended.

Finally, there is the point that working on the garden railway in the fresh air is a much more healthy occupation than crouching over a narrow shelf in a stuffy attic.

Climatic Conditions

Although the climate of the British Isles is often condemned by those who have to live in it, there are really very few places which are likely to be unsuitable for the successful running of a miniature garden railway. Various districts which suffer heavy rainfall will obviously limit the time that can be spent working on the railway and in some cases, it may be agreed that the climate is definitely against successful operation. For instance, the Lake District, the West Coast of Scotland and certain parts of West Wales are not really ideal as locations for the model garden railway. However, even these districts should not be ruled out by the enthusiast who is prepared to overcome certain drawbacks.

Sites

The ideal site for a garden railway is one which is comparatively level, though easy slopes or undulating ground are no disadvantage; in fact, some variation in level can be utilised to build interesting scenic features, embankments, cuttings, tunnels and so forth.

Gardens which are on a steep incline are obviously difficult to use for any kind of model railway, but by putting in a good deal of hard navvying work, such a site can still be utilised. Gradients on the model railway track should never exceed 1 in 50 and, in fact, if clockwork locomotives or electric trains of moderate power are to be run, gradients should be kept to no steeper than 1 in 80.

One important point should be remembered in planning a garden railway, and that is to lay the curved track to as large a radius as possible. As most model railway enthusiasts are only familiar with the usual indoor line, there is always the tendency to lay out the track to the very small radii which are inevitable on the indoor railway. But once in the garden, the railway builder should aim at laying his main line with radii more approximating to those used in full-size tracks. This question of track radius will be dealt with in Chapter 6.

Soils

The type of soil found in the garden will have a big effect on the building and successful operation of the garden railway. The ideal subsoil is gravel, while chalk gives reasonable conditions. Heavy clay soils are probably the worst because in wet weather they hold the water and make everything very damp, while in dry weather clay soils go very hard and crack. There are, of course, many ways of improving the subsoil which should not be overlooked. This will be dealt with in a later chapter.

Scales

The subject of the scale to be adopted for the miniature garden railway is obviously a highly controversial one as can be judged from the letters in the Model Railway Press. The first part of this book will only deal with what are usually called scenic railways, while lines which carry live passengers will be dealt with in the second part.

The two most popular scales for the scenic model railway in the garden are gauge "0" ($1\frac{1}{4}$ in. gauge or 32 mm.) and gauge "1" (10 mm. to the ft. scale and $1\frac{3}{4}$ in. gauge). At one time, 2 in. gauge was quite popular in this country and several garden railways were built to this size for which many fine models were available from the Trade. Between the two World Wars, 2 in. gauge died out and was replaced generally by a track gauge of $2\frac{1}{2}$ in. for which the scale for the rolling stock of $\frac{17}{32}$ in. = 1 ft. was adopted. But this larger size, especially with the rapid development in the design of the locomotives, is now considered too large and powerful for scenic work. At the same time, a $2\frac{1}{2}$ in. gauge locomotive, even if of a large type and coal-fired,

A view on the Gauge "0" garden railway of Mr. Featherstone of North Walsham.   Train leaving the indoor part of the line.

Work in progress on Mr. Featherstone's Gauge "0" garden railway: relaying sidings.

Another view of Mr. Featherstone's railway: note asbestos base on 3 in. x 1 in. timbers.

A fine Gauge "0" garden railway, with wooden construction.   (Photograph by courtesy of "Model Railway News".)

Another view of the Gauge "0" garden railway: G.W.R. 4–6–0 on passenger train (M.R.N.).

Gauge "0" North London 0–6–0 tank with twin articulated coach set. (M.R.N.).

This view shows the longitudinal battens and roofing felt between longitudinal planks and cross planks. (*M.R.N.*).

L.N.E.R. B.1 class 4–6–0 on train of teak coaches. (*M.R.N.*).

is not really suitable for consistent and reliable passenger hauling, and so in recent years, builders of passenger-carrying railways have adopted either 3½ in. gauge or 5 in. gauge, while enthusiasts who prefer to run their models on ground level now build for 7¼ in. gauge and even larger.

During the last few years, there has unfortunately been some fall in interest in gauge "o" and as a result, fewer finished models, parts, castings and so forth are available from the Trade. On the other hand, there are several companies now supplying parts for gauge "1" and with the valuable assistance which can be obtained from the Gauge "1" Association (a body formed a few years ago to popularise this larger size of railway), the gauge "1" line should be given careful consideration.

One big advantage of gauge "o" over its larger partner is that station platforms work out at very much shorter lengths and, of course, the radii of the curves on the main line can be made considerably smaller.

Supporters of gauge "1" claim that this size is ideal for use on garden railways, as powerful and efficient internally-fired steam locomotives can be built, while at the same time, clockwork or electric traction can be used with every success. They claim that steam is not altogether satisfactory in gauge "o", while clockwork is obviously ruled out in the larger scales.

A Mr. Victor Harrison of Bishops Stortford, writing in the magazine "Model Railway News", said "I think that gauge "1" is ideal for an outdoor scenic railway in all respects and I maintain that if only more publicity was accorded to the gauge, in the model technical journals, and if the Trade would respond by advertising gauge "1" products, it would once again be in the ascendant."

Since these words were written the Trade have certainly made some response and the supply position for gauge "1" components is now moderately satisfactory.

To return to gauge "o" with a scale of 7 mm. to the ft., there was at one time a huge variety of quite good models supplied by the Trade, but unfortunately, the great popularity of the very small scales has caused many of the model railway supply houses to abandon all production of gauge "o" components and to concentrate on the "oo" gauge and smaller. However, gauge "o" still has one advantage over gauge "1" and that is that (apart from the smaller space required) the essential components such as the electric motors for driving locomotives, wheels, axleboxes, etc., are considerably cheaper than similar parts for the larger scale.

Fine Scale Gauge "o"

In recent years, many gauge "o" enthusiasts have become dissatisfied with the rather coarse standards to which the gauge "o" models supplied by the Trade were being built and a new set of standards was introduced, generally known as the Gauge "o" Fine, where all the essential dimensions such as height and width of rail, wheel flange thickness and depth, and wheel back-to-back are considerably finer than in the ordinary gauge "o" standards —which are now generally called Gauge "o" Coarse Standards.

It was claimed at one time that the new gauge "o" Fine Standards would be quite unsuitable for garden railways, but this has been disproved by more than one enthusiast who have built quite large and highly successful outdoor railways using these finer standards.

The author suggests that the decision as to whether to adopt the gauge "o" Fine Standards or the Coarse Standards for a garden railway should be taken in light of the builder's skill in building his track and rolling stock, because quite clearly the Fine Standards call for a higher quality of workmanship and (perhaps more important) a higher standard of maintenance of the railway itself. One point may, however, be borne in mind and this is that although models built to the gauge "o" Coarse Standards may look rather clumsy and out of scale when viewed close up in a small room or even in an exhibition hall, these disadvantages are not nearly so apparent when the models are viewed in the garden.

Since the 1939/45 War, the British Railway Modelling Standards Bureau has been set up and has prepared a set of standards for model railway track, wheels and so forth and this has been done for both gauge "o" Coarse and gauge "o" Fine, and also for gauge "1" and the author strongly recommends that the garden railway builder adheres as closely as possible to these recommendations. The standards are as follows:—

Narrow Gauge Railways

If the builder of the model railway in the garden is a narrow gauge enthusiast, it is not a bad scheme to combine the many advantages of a larger scale with the existing gauge. At one time, there were many narrow gauge railways in the British Isles having gauges between 2 ft. and 3 ft. (such as the Lynton and Barnstaple, Leek and Manifold, Festiniog, Welshpool and Llanfair, Isle of Man, etc.) and one of these could be chosen as the prototype for the model railway running on gauge "o" track made to the Coarse standards. Probably the best way of dealing with the scale/gauge problem is to stick to the standard gauge (i.e. $1\frac{1}{4}$ in. or 32 mm.) and work out the correct scale to go with this gauge. There is a further advantage in the narrow gauge type of locomotive and this is that even if it is built exactly to scale, it will negotiate quite sharp curves.

A final thought on the problem of choosing the scale to be adopted. Even if the builder has both the time and skill to build all the rolling stock, track, etc., for the gauge "1" garden railway, the total cost is likely to be almost double that for an equivalent number of components built for gauge "o".

CHAPTER TWO

Track Layout

HAVING DECIDED ON THE SCALE to be used for the garden railway, the next step is to make a preliminary survey of the site to decide the general arrangement and position of the layout.

Model railways can generally be divided into two different types, the continuous and the non-continuous. There is, however, a most useful compromise between the two where a junction is made with a continuous track and the lines leading off are taken into a terminus station. The continuous track will obviously appeal to readers who build steam locomotives and like to demonstrate the capacity of their engines both on non-stop runs and on the hauling of heavy loads.

The continuous track, however, has certain limitations: it does not resemble full-size tracks and has little interest from the operating point of view. End to end working on a non-continuous line is much more realistic as full-size practice can then be followed, down to quite small details, though running on this type of line really calls for two operators.

A very good type of layout for the garden railway is one having a double track continuous main line with two or three double junctions leading off to a terminus which can very conveniently be accommodated in a small shed, an outhouse or even in one of the rooms in the house, according to one's facilities. Such a layout is an ideal one for a single operator and allows for interesting train operation in and around the terminus, in addition to continuous running on the main lines when required. An intermediate station or stations may be sited on the continuous part of the line, thus giving variety in the station buildings and rolling stock facilities.

Track Layout

If it is desired to run an intensive service on the garden line, a double track will be preferred, but a single line with passing loops can be very interesting to operate and is obviously much cheaper to instal.

At one time, the object in planning the model railway seemed to be to try and get the maximum amount of track into the minimum amount of space. Turnouts and crossings were made more and more complicated, single and double slips and scissors crossovers abounded and the whole trackwork became a signalman's nightmare. Another custom was to give high sounding titles such as King's Cross and Edinburgh to small single platform stations at short distances apart and served by four-coach trains!

11

The model railway enthusiasts of today, however, are treating this problem in a more sensible manner and keep the complication of the track within reasonable bounds. They build their stations more in proportion with the size of the line as a whole and name them more sensibly.

Modelling branch lines has become popular over the last few years for branch lines have the great advantage that it is possible to build stations which are quite close copies of their prototypes; the trackwork especially as regards carriage and wagon sidings and locomotive facilities can also be made reasonably close to the full-size article. Signalling too is far more practicable if the layout is a sensibly modest one and this should be particularly borne in mind on the garden railway where the alighting of a blackbird on the arm of a signal may be sufficient to upset the correct running of the trains.

The suggestion of siting a terminus station in a shed or outhouse has the big advantage that all the rolling stock on the line can be run in and left in the sidings or the platform roads where they are quite safe from the vagaries of the climate or from the predations of cats and dogs and other livestock. Being able to run the rolling stock into such a terminus also avoids that unrealistic and annoying chore of constantly carting the rolling stock to and from the house. To take full advantage of this scheme, the building housing the terminus station should be a sound weatherproof one with a proper floor, good ventilation and heated to a moderate temperature during the winter. If these conditions cannot be met, it is safer to take all rolling stock into the house for storage during the winter months or during spells when the railway is out of operation, for a cold, damp atmosphere can be very damaging to models, particularly those made of wood and cardboard.

Sheds

Many houses boast a shed of some sort which can be pressed into service for housing the terminus of the model railway; but in some cases, such sheds will be used for garden implements or other purposes and the builder of the railway may decide that the acquisition or construction of a new shed is desirable.

In such cases, the reader is advised to make enquiries regarding any Building By-laws in the district in which he resides. In some areas, there may be restrictions as to the construction of the shed and also as regards its siting in relation not only to the owner's own house but to the houses of neighbours. In some cases, the Town Planning Authorities are not very much concerned about the erection of small sheds provided that they are not unsightly and also that they do not spoil the view or hide the sunlight from the houses of one's neighbours. At all events, the wise model railway builder will consult both his neighbours and the appropriate authorities before taking any steps to acquire or construct his shed.

Perhaps a word on suitable sheds for the purpose of housing the terminus of a model garden railway will be of interest. Good quality timber is now extremely expensive and a quick look at the catalogues of the many manu-facturers of ready-made workshops and garages may give the impression that it is much cheaper to buy a commercially-made shed which is ready for erection rather than attempt to build the shed oneself. It should, however, be remembered that the lower-priced commercial portable buildings are generally made of rather thin materials and also almost certainly need to be lined on the inside with some kind of insulation, so as to make the heating of the shed in winter an economical proposition.

Generally speaking, the steel and asbestos type of shed is less convenient for the model builder as it is much easier to erect suitable shelving and supports for the trackwork inside a shed made entirely of wood. If the model railwayman does decide to build his own shed, the question of not only the internal lining of the walls but that of ventilation and lighting should be carefully gone into. While plenty of daylight is clearly desirable, it should not be forgotten that windows not only let in the sun, (which can be damaging if the sun is very hot and there are no blinds fitted) but that they also make the shed much harder to heat in the winter, unless the builder can afford double-glazing for all the windows. The floor should preferably be made of concrete to which some water-proofing agent such as Pudlo has been added and this may either be covered with a cheap quality flooring of some kind such as linoleum, or even an old carpet which has seen better days and is no longer good enough for the house. Concrete itself is much too cold to stand on in the winter.

The height of the trackwork inside the shed should be carefully con-sidered, for although it is nice to have the track at a good height from the floor in order to enjoy a realistic view of the railway, it may prove very diffi-cult to bring the main lines coming in from the garden up to this height. The solution to this problem will obviously depend on the levels in the garden itself.

The question of the height of the railway in the garden is a difficult one. If the track is laid on really high embankments (say 2 ft.) the line can be comfortably operated without much bending down, but it will not look very realistic and it also limits the builder to either timber or concrete foundations, unless rather expensive brickwork is adopted. On the other hand, actual ground level looks much more like the real railway, but it entails much backache when operating and can also lead to trouble with drainage. The author's advice, therefore, is to adopt a compromise wherever possible and his suggestion is between 8 in. and 12 in. from the ground level as a general rule, according to the levels in the garden itself.

Gradients and Curves

The gradients to be adopted on the model garden railway are important considerations. A dead level line is probably the best if clockwork loco-motives are going to be used, for even a slight gradient will reduce the speed of these and the sight of a model locomotive stalled is hardly a creditable one for the operator. A sharp radius curve will also reduce the hauling capacity of clockwork engines quite considerably, owing to the friction of the wheel flanges against the rails. The maximum gradients for clockwork locomotives for gauge "o" or "1" should not therefore be steeper than 1 in 100, while for steam locomotives this can be increased if necessary to about 1 in 60. Electric locomotives can generally negotiate rather steeper gradients and so a recommended maximum would be around 1 in 40.

The minimum radius of curved track for all types of gauge "o" locomotives should be about 8 ft. and for gauge "1" about 15 ft.

General Arrangements

It is important that a garden railway is laid in a permanent manner in such a way that it will blend with the general layout of the garden. It is generally best to arrange the track around or within reach of a lawn so that the line can be shown off to the best advantage and enabling visitors to move about to inspect the railway. The whole of the trackwork should be readily accessible and not placed in difficult positions behind large shrubs or close to a bed of valuable plants. Tunnels also should be particularly watched as when de-railments occur, these always have a nasty habit of happening inside the tunnel.

Sometimes the position of the garden in relation to the sun is a consideration, as a little shade may help to reduce track maintenance problems which arise from continual expansion and contraction of the rails. By careful planting of flowers, it is generally possible to arrange tall ones at the back and shorter plants in front of the track so that by careful arrangement, a pleasing and artistic effect can be obtained, and the model railway will not interfere with enjoyment of the garden in its own right.

The use of small hedges or bushes such as box and privet should not be despised, especially the latter which is very quick growing and can, therefore, be clipped as and when required. Where proper embankments are required, a good quality lawn grass should be sown and this should be kept well weeded at regular intervals. It will also have to be cut very close to give anything like a scale effect.

CHAPTER THREE

Foundations

BEFORE STARTING THE ACTUAL CONSTRUCTION of a garden railway, a reasonably accurate layout plan should be prepared and this should be drawn to scale on large sheets of cartridge paper or something equally strong. On the plan, the position of all buildings, trees and shrubs should be clearly marked and some attempt should be made to determine the levels at different points of the line.

If the garden is on a severe slope, the difference in level at one end of the railway to another should be carefully measured as shown in fig. 1 or this can be done very accurately by the use of the garden hose and two lengths of transparent tubing (either glass or plastic).

It is a good plan to start the actual foundations of the railway in October, for at that time of the year there is less risk of damaging growing plants and, in fact, most of the plants in the garden will be starting to shed their leaves so that the site will generally be much more accessible than in the spring or summer. Work should start by laying out the centre line of the railway by setting out a row of pegs at definite distances apart, say 3 ft., and if the section of line is to be laid dead level, this can be achieved by using a large spirit level laid on the edge of a straight piece of board.

Gradients can be dealt with as follows. Suppose the gradient is 1 in 100. This is equivalent to a rise of 1 ft. in 100 ft. which is approximately equivalent to a rise of $\frac{1}{3}$ in. in 3 ft. Thus, if the board carrying the spirit level is first temporarily laid so that it is exactly horizontal by the level, by raising one end of the board by $\frac{1}{3}$ in., the desired gradient will be achieved.

Foundations

Dealing first with track which is laid on the ground, there are two principle ways in arranging for the foundations. The first is to follow approximately the method used in full-size railways, which is to excavate for a reasonable depth, to lay first coarse ballast and then fine ballast on top of this, into which the sleepers are set. Drainage arrangements must, of course, be made and these will depend on the type of soil. If the soil is a light one with a gravel subsoil, all the builder will need to do is to consolidate the soil under the foundations by a little ramming. A clay or loam soil will require artificial draining arrangements. A clay soil can be bored, after ramming, about every 2 ft. or so along the centre line of the railway, the holes then being filled up with broken bricks, cinders or clinkers. If the ground is exceptionally wet, a

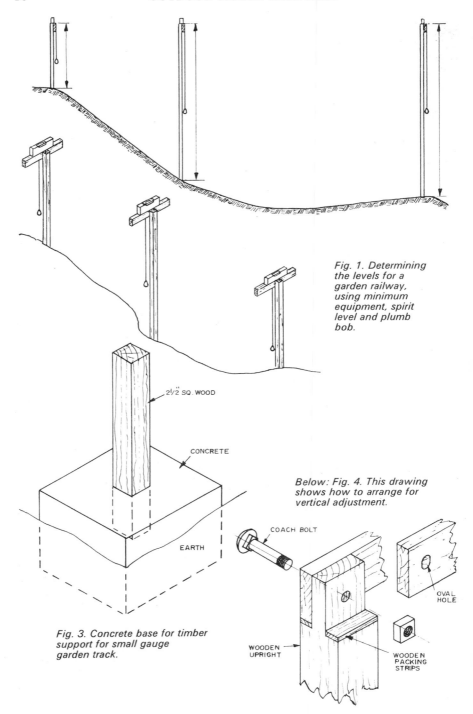

Fig. 1. Determining
the levels for a
garden railway,
using minimum
equipment, spirit
level and plumb
bob.

2½″ SQ. WOOD

CONCRETE

Below: Fig. 4. This drawing
shows how to arrange for
vertical adjustment.

COACH BOLT

EARTH

OVAL
HOLE

Fig. 3. Concrete base for timber
support for small gauge
garden track.

WOODEN
UPRIGHT

WOODEN
PACKING
STRIPS

Gauge "0" L.M.S. "Princess" Pacific on mail train.   The line is electrified on the centre third-rail system.   (M.R.N.).

A view of M. Ritz's Gauge "0" outdoor line under construction.   (Photograph by the author.)

Another view of M. Ritz's outdoor railway in Paris. (Photograph by the author.)

This view of M. Ritz's line shows some of the pointwork. Electrification on the overhead system was added later. (Photograph by the author.)

more elaborate continuous drain may be dug alongside the line and about 1 ft. deep, this being filled as before with a light top layer of ballast for appearance's sake.

A second method of arranging for the foundations of the garden railway is by laying old roofing slates on edge at a suitable distance apart, the slates being held upright by means of stakes or even small rods. The trough so formed between the slates is then filled in as described previously.

Another method is to use a complete concrete trough as shown in fig. 2. The trough must be provided with proper drainage holes and planed wooden bearers will be required to carry the longitudinal battens on which the sleepers are laid. If this method is adopted, it is a good plan to cast holes of suitable size in one edge of the trough into which hard wood dowels may be inserted to carry signal wire guides or point rodding guides. The precast concrete troughs may be cast in lengths of 3 to 4 ft. and some means should be arranged in the shuttering to align the ends of adjoining sections.

Timber foundations are almost certainly the most popular for small gauge railways. They can be used whether the track is just above the ground level or 3 to 4 ft. above it. For gauge "o" and gauge "1" railways, the verticals should be at least $2\frac{1}{2}$ in. square and should have a foot made as shown in fig. 3 to give additional stability. All timber used in foundations should be

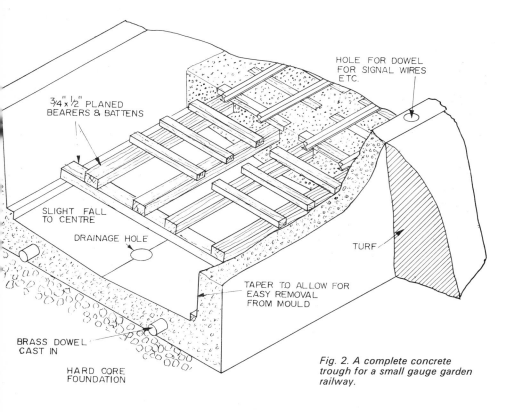

HOLE FOR DOWEL FOR SIGNAL WIRES ETC.

3/4" x 1/2" PLANED BEARERS & BATTENS

SLIGHT FALL TO CENTRE

DRAINAGE HOLE

TURF

TAPER TO ALLOW FOR EASY REMOVAL FROM MOULD

BRASS DOWEL CAST IN

HARD CORE FOUNDATION

Fig. 2. A complete concrete trough for a small gauge garden railway.

thoroughly soaked in creosote or some other wood preservative and it is a good plan to set the foot of all such supports into concrete to minimise rotting. In the composition of the concrete, water-proofing agent, such as Pudlo, should be added. The part of the timber upright which is most likely to be affected by rotting is generally that where it enters the ground, so it is not a bad plan to bring the top of the concrete a little above ground level and slope it away in all directions from the timber.

The tops of the timber uprights should be so shaped that the longitudinal members can be attached to them with ready adjustment for height. This can be achieved by using an oval slot through the upright and a coach bolt right through both the longitudinals and the uprights. Another method is to use packing strips underneath the lower edge of the longitudinals as shown in fig. 4.

Before laying the track itself, some form of flat baseboard may be laid on the longitudinals to which the track battens can be screwed. A good material for this baseboard is standard asbestos sheet. It will be found that self-tapping screws can be put into this material without difficulty. Although some model railways of this type have been laid with the sleepers resting directly on the baseboard, it will be found much more satisfactory to use the conventional longitudinal battens, especially on curved track. The sleepers can be pinned to the battens and here it is a good idea to use alternate brass and steel pins. Although steel pins may rust in time they do not come out, whereas brass pins have a nasty habit of jumping out due to variations in the weather.

If the system is an electric one, consideration should be given at an early stage to the method of wiring. If the stud-contact system is to be adopted (and this system is strongly recommended for garden railways) the railway can easily be spoilt by the sight of the connecting wire which has to be laid right along the track to connect to the studs or pins. Probably the best method of avoiding this difficulty is to use studs which are long enough to pass right through the sleeper and to wire them up on the underside of the length of track before laying the track on the baseboard. Thus after the final ballasting has been carried out, all trace of the wiring will be hidden.

When designing the baseboard of the track, the builder should not forget the various wider sections which will be required for the station buildings, signals and other line-side accessories.

CHAPTER FOUR

Viaducts, Bridges and Tunnels

ONE OF THE BIG ADVANTAGES of a garden model railway is the possibility of building realistic engineering works such as viaducts, bridges and tunnels. They can easily be constructed of durable and weather-resisting materials, though wood that has been well-treated in preservative should not be despised.

Reinforced Concrete Viaducts

Reinforced concrete is, of course, the obvious material for model viaducts, and structures made of this material, properly designed, will last a lifetime. A start should be made by preparing an accurate scale drawing of the complete viaduct, after which the shuttering for casting the various sections should be designed. A simple type of shuttering is shown in fig. 5. The shuttering should be thoroughly greased before use to prevent the mix sticking to it after the concrete has set. As to the reinforcing material, this must obviously depend on the depth of the concrete itself and the general shape of the structure, but lengths of thick iron wire or possibly odd lengths of small diameter round or flat steel strip from the workshop scrap box can all be pressed into service. A suggestion as to how the reinforcing wires or rods should be arranged is shown in fig. 6. The mixing of the concrete should be carried out with care and a good proportion is 4 parts of good sharp sand to 1 part of Portland cement with a small proportion of Pudlo. When the mixture has been thoroughly stirred and in a nice flowing condition but not too "runny", it should be poured into the shuttering and well prodded to ensure that it reaches all of the corners in the detail work. A bricklayer's trowel will be found useful to finish off the top of the arch.

The whole must now be left until the concrete is thoroughly set; during this time it should be slightly wetted at intervals to prevent too rapid drying out. This process may take two or even three days, after which the screws holding the shuttering together can be removed. If there are any "blow holes" which show on the surface, these should be filled up using the trowel and it is a good plan to scrape such holes out at the back to form a key so that the additional concrete cannot come away when it dries.

If the shuttering is suitably designed, the ends of each section of viaduct can be made to interlock so that they will not come apart after they have been laid into position. The ballasting can then be carried out, this being brought up to just below the top so as to form a parapet. The track is now

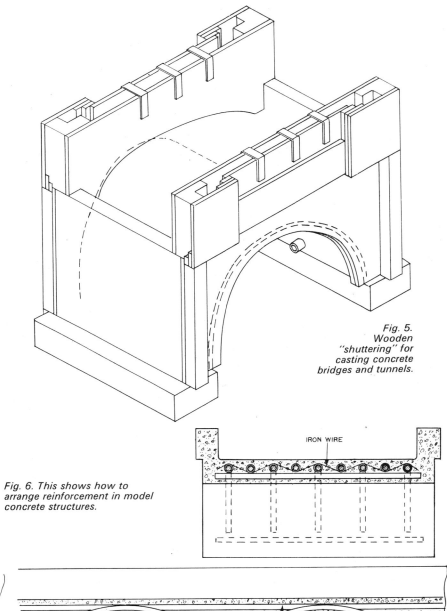

Fig. 5.
Wooden
"shuttering" for
casting concrete
bridges and tunnels.

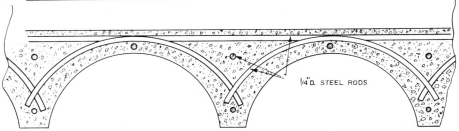

IRON WIRE

Fig. 6. This shows how to
arrange reinforcement in model
concrete structures.

¼" D. STEEL RODS

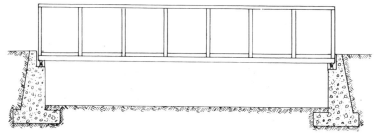

Fig. 7. A steel plate girder bridge.

set into this ballast and a final shallow layer of "scale" ballast laid between the sleepers.

An important point to remember in all model concrete work is that any recesses or holes required in the concrete should be formed before the concrete has set, as it is practically impossible to chip out holes for signals or electrical equipment at a later date.

Bridges

Full-size railway bridges are today made either in reinforced concrete or built up from steel sections; but in earlier days, wood bridges were quite common, especially in Cornwall and abroad and many of these wooden structures make magnificent prototypes for models.

All wooden bridges should be constructed of planed yellow pine or if this cannot be obtained, obechi or oak are quite good substitutes. All parts should be screwed together using brass wood screws or in some cases, metal screws such as 4 or 6 BA. There is such an enormous variety of steel railway bridges that the author does not propose to discuss these in detail, but will merely mention the most suitable method of construction, in model size. Brass channel section and I girders and also angles of all sizes and thicknesses can

Fig. 8. A "N" type lattice girder bridge, showing arrangement of components.

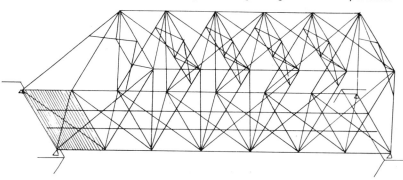

be obtained in brass and these should be bolted together using brass screws and then sweated over with soft solder. Some basic designs of steel bridges are given in figs. 7 and 8.

Tunnels

No model railway ever seems complete without a tunnel and if there are any children in the family, a tunnel will definitely be insisted upon. In garden railways, tunnels can however become rather a nuisance, for as mentioned previously, if a derailment does occur it always seems to occur in the middle of the tunnel. On indoor railways it is usually easy to arrange for the top of the tunnel to be hinged to give immediate access to the track, but this is clearly not so easy in the garden. The answer is to keep the tunnels only for straight track and not to make them so long that one cannot extricate derailed rolling stock or remove any foreign bodies which may tend to collect there. It should not be forgotten that some animals may make use of the tunnel for their afternoon nap. The structure to form the tunnel proper can be built up quite easily out of ordinary bricks or a fairly large diameter drainpipe can be considered for a gauge "o" railway. The outer covering of the tunnel will, of course, consist of earth covered with grass or plants as required; the entrances provide the builder with an interesting exercise in design for these should be built to scale for the sake of appearance. The reader is commended to the beautiful designs of tunnel entrances on the former Great Western Railway such as those at Box and Twerton which were designed by the famous engineer, I. K. Brunel.

CHAPTER V

Stations and Station Buildings

FOR MODEL PURPOSES, the author suggests that the station buildings on the garden railway should be based on actual full-size designs. In this way, the resulting structures will provide an added interest and convey a flavour appropriate to the railway company being modelled.

To make a start on the station platforms, one of the best materials for these is asbestos sheeting which can be laid on top of either wooden battens or concrete sections, the asbestos sheet being allowed to overlap the battens slightly on the side adjoining the track. If concrete is used, this should again be mixed up from 1 part of Portland cement and 4 of sharp sand and for a realistic appearance, the sides of the concrete sections can be scribed so as to represent the blocks used in the full-size platforms. It should not be forgotten that any holes required for wooden dowels or for the siting of vertical awning supports or pillars or station lamps should be provided for before the concrete has set.

Although wood can be used for station platforms, if it is made of sections reasonably close to scale, there is sure to be trouble from warping sooner or later, especially in damp situations.

The disadvantage of wood as a material for station work does not necessarily apply to the actual buildings and wood is certainly an easier material in which to incorporate all the complicated detail work of the full-size building. All wood should be thoroughly soaked in creosote or a good preservative before use and as an additional protection, two or three coats of a good quality enamel are suggested. Some of the detail work can be done in metal, such as brass sections for gutters and valances, window sills and door handles, and all such sections should be firmly attached to the buildings with fine brass wood screws. Roofs of all buildings will, of course, have to be made thoroughly watertight and for this purpose one of the many roofing materials on the market should be suitable.

As regards the sides of the buildings, it is almost impossible to score the wood to represent scale brickwork, so the best alternative here is to assume that the prototype building is of timber construction so that all planking can be straightforward vertical or horizontal lines. Plenty of internal "walls" should be provided, not only to represent the various rooms in the station building, but to stiffen the whole building and to prevent sagging in between the corners.

Another material suitable for roofs of model buildings is metal such as aluminium or zinc or even brass, though the high price of the last-mentioned material is rather against its frequent use. Brass has, however, the advantage that details such as gutters and rainwater pipes can be soldered.

Windows

If the material of which the sides of the building is made is not too thick, glass can be placed behind the wall overlapping the actual window opening and can be held in place by a simple framework made of wood. The glass for this purpose should be at least $\frac{1}{8}$ in. thick and most builders should not have much trouble in cutting the glass themselves.

Another method of fitting the window glass, more suitable where the wall thickness is rather great, is to cut the glass actually to the size of the opening and insert it almost flush with the outside; this, of course, calls for much more accurate glass cutting.

The actual cutting of the glass is done as follows. A flat, solid surface is chosen and this is covered with a piece of baize or a similar material, the glass is laid on this and a steel straight edge is put across the glass, measured for position and firmly held down. An ordinary wheel-type glass cutter is then pressed on hard at the start of the cut and is then drawn firmly along the straight edge for the full width of the glass. The glass cutter will make a crackling noise as it cuts into the glass and should leave a neat line right across. The sheet of glass is then shifted so that the line of the cut is exactly in line with the edge of a table or something equally flat and the overhanging part of the glass which is not required is then pressed firmly until the glass breaks off along the line.

Station Decorations

The appropriate notice boards typical to the British railway station, such as Booking Office, Waiting Room, Station Master's Office, Porters, etc., should not be passed over, as it is these little touches which make the whole set-up realistic. All such notice boards should either be made of brass sheet or of a good quality thin hardwood and should be painted with oil colours, a good quality coach varnish being used over the lettering, to preserve it from the elements. Another material quite suitable for these notice boards is thin opaque perspex; this should be slightly roughened with fine emery cloth before attempting to paint it. Notice boards should be firmly pinned on with small brass pins and so arranged that they can be easily removed from the model building for cleaning and repainting.

Station Lighting

If it is intended to operate the garden model railway at night, (and this can be extremely interesting in good weather) it is well worth while to instal lighting in the stations and signal boxes. It is possible to obtain low voltage electric bulbs almost to scale size for gauge "o" and good use can be made

A fine achievement by A. A. Sherwood of Sydney, Australia: a Gauge "0" steam-driven Mallet locomotive. Track on longitudinal timbers with brick uprights.

A 3½ in. Gauge ground-level line in Germany, built by F. Grosse-Holtfort.

A view of the steaming bays at a meeting of the New Jersey (U.S.A.) Live Steamers. The stock are 3½ in. and 4¾ in. gauges. (Photograph—Conrad Milster.)

A view of the 3½ in. Gauge line of Al Millburn, Connecticut, U.S.A. Note deep section rail. (Photograph—D. H. Downie.)

A ground-level line in Germany: Adolf Lallinger of Pasing, near Munich, prepares for a run with his 0–6–0 tank locomotive, which is fitted with Allan valve gear.

An American "Ten-Wheeler" on the New Jersey railroad. Flat-bottom rail on wooden superstructure. (Photograph—Conrad Milster.)

Another example of a raised permanent track with wooden longitudinals and flat bottom rail. The rail appears to be very light in section for passenger carrying. The locomotive is a most unusual type, one of the early Camelbacks, built by Mr. G. R. Thomas of Havertown, Pennsylvania.

A view of the old Chingford track; steel flats were used for the rails, and concrete longitudinals and uprights. The late H. J. Turpin is at the controls of the Society's 4–4–2 locomotive "Firefly". (Photograph—C. B. Capener.)

of these fitted to lamp-posts along the platforms, while larger low voltage bulbs such as 6 volt car sidelight bulbs could be used to light the buildings themselves. The wiring for station lighting should be done using well-insulated electric wire and the various bulbs should be wired up in parallel so that all the lights do not go out if one lamp happens to fail. Provision must always be allowed for the wires to come up through the baseboard or through the embankment as the case may be, and then fed through the platform and brought out through holes drilled in the platform into which the lamps are fitted.

Signal Boxes

Quite a large proportion of the signal boxes used by the older railway companies were of wooden construction and these are probably the easiest to model, rather than the more recent brick-built structures. As most of the signal boxes on the model railway will not be dummies, but will actually provide shelter from the weather for the various lever frames required for the operation of points and signals, they should be strongly constructed and arranged with at least the back wall or possibly the back wall and half of the roof to be hinged to give access to the levers. It is a good plan to provide a track diagram with the appropriate points and signals numbered, which can be attached to the hinged part of the signal box wall, so that when this is opened the operator has this in front of him while he is pulling the various levers.

CHAPTER SIX

Track and Track Laying

AS MENTIONED IN CHAPTER I, fine scale gauge "o" track is not necessarily ruled out when laid out of doors, providing that the builder is prepared to devote a reasonable amount of time to maintenance work; but most gauge "o" enthusiasts will probably make their first attempt in the garden with the standard gauge "o" track materials.

The first point to be decided is the type of track parts to be used and here the choice seems to rest between brass or nickel-silver rail, using die-cast chairs if the rail is of the bullhead section, or the usual dog spikes if the rail is flat bottomed. Steel rail is not to be recommended, as although this is usually sheradised, this finishing process does not generally keep the rust at bay for any length of time, and once rust has got a grip, steel rails will deteriorate very rapidly. In any case, if steel rail were used for the making up of points, the blades and frogs will have to be filed, thus removing the protective coating, so that they would have a very short life indeed.

Although chairs with wooden keys are sometimes suggested for use with bullhead rail, they are not recommended for outdoor use as the keys are either too tight or too loose, according to the humidity of the atmosphere, so that the platelayer is likely to spend a great deal of time putting back wooden keys that have fallen out. Again the pressed-steel slide-on chairs which were popular at one time cannot be recommended for the outdoor railway. They rust very quickly and as they are made of rather thin material, their life is very short. Chairs for bullhead rail, therefore, should be of the slide-on variety with a key incorporated in the casting.

Returning to the question of whether to use nickel-silver or brass rail, the former is much more realistic due to its almost white colour and it does not tend to corrode as quickly as brass, thus being better as a conductor of electricity. It is, however, considerably more expensive than brass, so the choice of these two metals will be one for the constructor to take at the outset.

Although the standard gauge "o" track parts are mostly made today to the recommendations of the British Railway Modelling Standards Bureau, at the time of writing, there still appears to be some variation in rail height. The higher section of rail might be used for a gauge "I" railway while the smaller section is suggested for gauge "o".

Sleepers and Battens

The sleepers for the garden railway do not need to be any larger than those normally used for indoor model railways, that is to say, for standard gauge "o" track 3 in. long by $\frac{3}{8}$ in. by $\frac{1}{4}$ in. and for scale track, $2\frac{1}{2}$ in. long by $\frac{1}{4}$ in. by $\frac{1}{8}$ in. They should be thoroughly soaked in creosote before laying and it is recommended that the normal longitudinal battens should be used. The spikes to hold the sleepers down onto the battens should be half of brass and half of steel. This is because, as mentioned previously, when used out of doors, brass spikes have a tendency to jump out. Sometimes track builders dispense with the use of battens; but if this is done, it will be found much more difficult to make small adjustments to the level or alignment of the track than if the track is laid on the regulation battens. Battens also have the additional advantage that curved track can be made up in a jig and the battens will, of course, hold the rails and sleepers at the desired radius after the finished track is lifted from the jig.

If the track is being laid direct onto a wooden foundation, fairly small brass wood screws can be used, not put through the sleepers but through the battens only. If the track bed is an asbestos one, it will be found that small self-tapping screws as used in motor car bodywork are quite satisfactory.

As mentioned previously, jigs can be made up for curved track and in fact jigs are also useful when constructing ordinary straight track. Such a jig is shown in fig. 9 and is best made in hardwood and then ribbed underneath to prevent warping.

The actual construction of straight track is very simple. The battens are first cut to length and laid between the spacers in the bottom of the jig, the

Fig. 9. A hardwood jig
for track making.

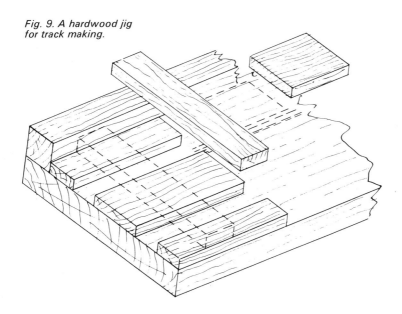

sleepers being then pinned down at the required spacing, the pins being put in in such a position that they will be covered by the rail when this is later pinned down. This will ensure that the spikes used in the chairs will not foul the heads of the pins holding the sleepers down.

If the battens are about $\frac{1}{4}$ in. thick (as is often the case) the pins used to hold the sleepers to them should be of sufficient length to allow their ends to be turned over and clinched with a hammer.

When the sleepering operation is complete, two lengths of rail are taken and the lower part of each end filed slightly thinner so as to assist sliding on the chairs. To enable the chairs to be threaded on the rail without difficulty, a hardwood block with a raised stop can be used so that a chair can be laid in front of it and the rail pushed through each time until sufficient chairs for the length of the rail are in position. The builder is warned to watch that the chairs are put on the rail the same way round, for the outside of a railway chair is always different from the inside.

The chairs are now spaced out roughly by hand to correspond with the spacing of the sleepers and the rail length placed in position. Another spacer can be used to get this first rail in the right place, measuring from one edge of the sleepers. Track spikes are now put in the chairs at the extreme ends and in about two or three other sleepers in between so as to hold the rail roughly in position. The rail can then be "sighted" to make sure that it is dead straight and any slight adjustments are then made by gently tapping the chair that is out of line into position with a piece of soft wood. The remaining spikes can then be driven home and it is best to drive them half-way home with a hammer and then finish driving them with a hollow punch, which will prevent any damage to the chairs in the event of the hammer slipping. As recommended previously, the spikes holding down the chairs should be partly steel and partly brass. The second rail is then laid by means of a track gauge (as shown in fig. 10) and the pinning down process is carried out as for the first rail.

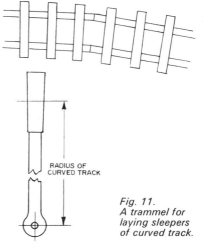

Fig. 10. A simple track gauge.

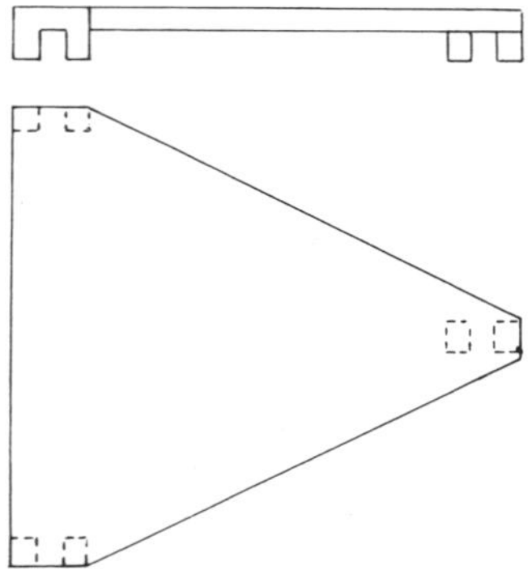

RADIUS OF
CURVED TRACK

Fig. 11.
A trammel for
laying sleepers
of curved track.

Curved Track

The building of curved track is a little more complicated and it is generally made in 18 in. lengths rather than 3 ft. lengths as on straights, so as to enable ordinary straight battens to be used. If jigs are to be used for making curved track, it is sensible to standardise on not more than two radii for the curves. Even this means that four jigs will be required if the layout includes any double track as there will be a measurable difference of radius between the inner and outer line. To ensure that the jigs for curved track are reasonably accurate, a trammel should be made up and used to mark out the lines of the outer and inner ends of the sleepers while the trammel may also be fitted with a metal track gauge to ensure that the rails themselves are also pinned down to the correct radius. If space permits, a long piece of timber may be firmly screwed to the underside of the curved track jig and the trammel set up permanently on this as shown in fig. 11, and the outer end of the trammel can then be used to ensure that the sleepers are laid at the correct angle relative to the track.

When cutting the rails for curved track, it should not be forgotten that the inner rail will always be a little shorter than the outer rail according to the radius of the curve. (The difference is approximately $\frac{1}{2}$ in. on a 6 ft. radius curve).

Some builders prefer to use a drawing or blueprint for curved track and in this case the print itself can be pinned down with drawing pins, the battens and sleepers cut to the lengths shown on the drawing and pinned down on top. The outer rail of the curved track should be laid first and if the track gauge shown in fig. 10 is used, it must be arranged with the double guide on the outside rail and with the single guide on the inner rail; this will ensure that the gauge of the track is very slightly increased according to the radius of the curve.

Some builders prefer to spring the rail when laying it to the desired radius but while this may be satisfactory where the rail section is a light one, for the standard gauge "o" and gauge "I" rails, it is advisable to bend the rail by hand to slightly less than the desired radius, the extreme ends of which rail being bent to a slightly smaller radius than the middle part.

Fishplates should be used for all rail joints and these should also be made of brass rather than steel. They should not, however, be relied upon for electrical contact if the railway is an electric one. The transmission of the current should be made certain by soldering a short length of thick copper wire onto the end of each adjoining section.

Pointwork

Although some track builders make up jigs for constructing turnouts or crossovers, they are not by any means essential if the following procedure is adopted: the lines of the rails are marked out on the baseboard and the straight and curved stock rails are then laid to the lines drawn out, allowing sufficient gaps in the chairs for the insertion of slide chairs or alternatively brass strip of such a section that it can be slid underneath the rail. The stock rails should either be joggled or filed to receive the sharp ends of the point blades and this must, of course, be done before laying them on the sleepers. After this the frog of the turnout is made up, the end of the short straight section being filed at the required angle and the short curved section butted up against it. Great care must be taken to ensure the correct gauge at the point of the frog.

The two point blades and wing rails are next taken in hand and the sharp ends of the blades filed up; the extreme ends of the blades should be shaped as shown in fig. 13. These are now laid, care being taken to get the frog ends accurately lined up with the frog itself, otherwise the backs of the wheels of the rolling stock may catch the wings or the check-rails. The final operation is the laying of the two check rails and the outer ends of these should be neatly lined up with the ends of the wing rails. The ends of the check rails should not be bent at too severe a radius, otherwise when the wheel flanges strike them, the rolling-stock may become derailed.

As mentioned earlier, it is not wise to build too much complicated point-work for use out of doors, but trailing or facing crossovers are perfectly satisfactory as these are, or course, virtually two turnouts laid end-to-end. If a little complication is desired, the single-slips can be considered, but double-slips should be avoided whenever possible as where the rail is of out-of-scale section, difficulty may be encountered in obtaining enough clearance for the movement of the outer ends of the blades.

The method of attachment of the ends of the point blades may sometimes cause trouble and the author recommends brass strip of fairly substantial section securely soldered to the blades; it should be possible to build up a nice fillet of solder on the "running" side of the blade, but the stock rail side must be completely free of solder or the blade will not close properly into the stock rail.

Points and crossovers should normally be arranged on a reasonably level stretch of baseboard and facing points on main lines should be avoided.

Ballasting

The final appearance of the track will depend a great deal on neat ballasting. Probably the most effective ballast for both gauge "o" and gauge "1"

Fig. 13. The correct shape for the ends of point blades.

Fig. 12. Bonding of rail ends for electric railways.

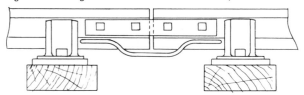

railways is ⅛ in. graded granite chippings; if this can be obtained direct from a local quarry, this material can be quite cheap, but if bought in small quantities in a district removed from any quarry it may be rather expensive and as an alternative, small washed gravel may be considered. Gravel can generally be obtained from the local builders' merchant and it should be reasonably free from sand or dust, otherwise it will not drain rainwater satisfactorily and will thus shorten the life of sleepers, battens and other woodwork. Gravel for ballasting can always be washed by agitating it in a large bowl of water, when any sand or dust present will sink to the bottom.

The top layer of ballast may be mixed with creosote and should then be laid in position to a level just below the top of the sleepers and nicely sloped off on the outsides of the track.

Super-elevation

Whether super-elevation or cant is required will depend on the radius of curved track. Generally speaking, it is not essential on radii over 7 ft. in "o" gauge or 9 ft. in gauge "1". For radii less than 7 ft. the sleepers may be canted by an amount equal to $\frac{1}{16}$ in. at the outer end. This can be done on a ballasted track merely by raking out ballast from underneath the sleepers in exactly the same manner as is done in full-size railway practice, whilst on timber foundations any super-elevation required can be provided by inserting short wooden wedges.

CHAPTER SEVEN

Signalling

ALTHOUGH IT MIGHT BE THOUGHT that signals in a garden railway are likely to be too fragile to stand up to normal conditions, they add so much to the character of the railway that they should not be overlooked. Most of the pre-grouping railways used distinctive types of signals of their own design and the "Big Four", with the exception of the Great Western Railway, adopted the well-known upper-quadrant signal. Later again, the railways adopted coloured light signals for many locations and these can also be modelled with great success, especially in the larger scales.

It is not proposed here to deal with the many types of signals in detail, but the reader is referred to an excellent series of articles by Mr. O. S. Nock which appeared in *Model Engineering* during 1940. These included scale drawings of many of the pre-grouping railway signals, together with much useful information.

The first part of the signal to consider is the post and many of the pre-grouping railways used a plain wooden post. While this is easy enough to get in model sizes, wood is not the ideal material to stand up to the British climate and a good alternative material is brass which can be obtained in a suitable square section and tapered in the usual way towards the finial.

If wooden posts are used, they should be made of teak for preference, though oak or beech are reasonable alternatives. The wood should be well rubbed down and given an undercoat and at least two top coats of white lead paint.

Some signals used tubular metal posts and these are easily copied using brass tube or rod of suitable diameter. The metal lattice posts used by some of the railways are much more difficult to make, but are most attractive in appearance. The best way to make a lattice post is to make up a simple jig of hardwood to hold the various brass sections in the required positions and at the required angles while they are soldered, using the ordinary soft solder and liquid flux.

The signal arms can sometimes be purchased ready-made complete with coloured transparent spectacles from the model supply houses, but they are not at all difficult to make using brass or nickel-silver sheet about $\frac{1}{32}$ in. thick for gauge "o" or gauge "1" railways. Red, blue and amber perspex can be obtained for making the spectacles; the blue colour combining with the yellowish effect of the electric bulb (if the signal is wired for electricity) will produce the characteristic bluish-green colour for the "all-clear" position.

32

An American "Ten-Wheeler" in 3½ in. gauge, built by A. W. Leggett of St. Lambert, P.Q., Canada. Steel angle rails on wooden sleepers.

A ground-level line for 3½ in. and 5 in. gauge in South Africa. The locomotive is to the "Caribou" design, built by Mrs. Yvette Etter.

Another view of the New Jersey railroad, showing a Reading "Pacific" and a Mallet in the background.

A view on the track of the North London Society of Model Engineers. This track uses wooden longitudinals and concrete uprights. Mr. Hatherill is seen driving Bill Carter's Great Northern "Atlantic". The signal on the left is a full-size somersault signal from the old Great Northern Railway. (Photograph—G. M. Cashmore.)

A portable steel track belonging to the Guildford Model Engineering Society.

Mr. Harold Pill inspecting G. M. Cashmore's 5 in. gauge "George V" at the North London Society's track at Colney Heath. The track is laid on wooden longitudinals with concrete uprights. (Photograph—G. M. Cashmore.)

Another view of the steaming bays at a meeting of the New Jersey live steamers. (*Photograph—Conrad Milster.*)

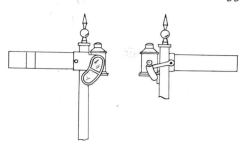

Fig. 14. Details of a "home"
signal, showing arm spectacles,
lamp, backshade and finial.

The bearing for the signal arm can be quite easily made from brass tube soldered direct to a metal signal post or if the post is a wooden one, soldered to a little plate which can be held to the post by two small wood screws, one above and one below the tubular bearing. A short length of brass wire or rod is soldered to the back of the signal arm to provide the pivot and the backshade is attached to this as shown in fig. 14.

The lever and balance weight which is usually but not always fitted near the base of the signal post may be made to scale, but if so, it will probably require a small tension spring to ensure that the arm is returned to the danger position on release of the control wire from the signal cabin. This is because of the additional friction which is generally present in any wiring parts used out of doors.

Siting of Signals

The correct position for signals on a railway is governed by established signalling rules and if it is desired to signal the layout correctly, quite a lot

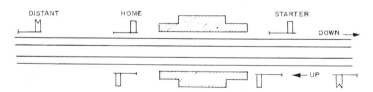

Fig. 15. Basic signalling for a simple station layout.

Below: Fig. 16. Signalling for a double junction.

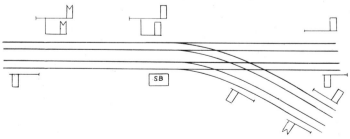

of signals will be required even for a fairly simple layout. It would take a great deal of space to discuss the various rules which govern the location of signals but the more important or basic signals required for a simple layout can be taken from figs. 15 and 16.

Signals should always be positioned so that the imaginary driver of the train can see them in sufficient time to follow their indication. This applies not only to the positioning of the signal arm in relation to the track it serves but also to the height of the arm from rail level. In many locations a white sighting-board behind the arm is an important and easily installed addition.

If a station is on a curve, very likely the driver will not be able to see his starter signal until he is half-way along the platform. In such a case a repeater signal can be fitted on or close to the platform at some point on its length.

Ground signals, either of the arm or disc type, are very attractive additions to the layout and as they can generally be made to work with the points they serve, they are not at all difficult to fit up.

Gantry signals make most attractive models, but if there are more than four arms on the one gantry, they will require quite a bit of ingenuity in arranging for positive control and they are also likely to need a fair amount of servicing when used out of doors.

Methods of Operation

The traditional round wire pulling direct on the signal through a series of guides is quite satisfactory on outdoor model railways providing that the parts are made a little over-scale and there are not too many cranks or pulleys between the signal and the lever frame. The best wire to use for manual operation of signals is a plain stainless steel wire and brass angle drilled with the required number of holes is quite satisfactory for the guides. The holes drilled in the guides should be made quite an easy fit for the wire used and should be lightly countersunk on both sides to reduce friction. They should be soldered to brass plates which should be rigidly attached by brass wood screws to suitable blocks of hardwood which are screwed in turn to the track battens. These wooden blocks should be at such a height that they can be lightly covered with fine ballast for appearance's sake.

The routing of the signal wires should be done with care before installing any guides, as the easiest route with the minimum number of bell-cranks or pulleys (which may not necessarily be the shortest route) should be chosen. Additional light tension springs may be installed at various points in the wire where the distance between the signal and its signal box is great.

Where the signals are to be lit up using the usual low voltage miniature bulbs, it is a good plan to run the live wire through copper or brass tube which can be hidden alongside the battens immediately underneath the sleepers; this will ensure that the wires are not interfered with during ordinary maintenance operations.

Another method for operating signals and points is by means of air pressure conveyed to them through small bore copper tubing. A small pneumatic cylinder is placed under the arm of the lever in the signal box and the lever is attached to a piston which is a close fit in the cylinder and fitted with a cup washer or an "O" ring. A similar fitting is connected to the signal or point at the other end of the pipeline. On pulling the lever in the signal box the piston moves in the signal box cylinder, increasing the pressure of the air in the pipe and thus moving the piston at the other end. When the lever in the signal box is replaced, the air is sucked back through the pipe and the signal arm is returned to the danger position. This system has been used in several well-known garden railways, but its success depends on good fitting pistons and suitable sizes for the pneumatic cylinders in the signal box and on the signals. For most small gauge garden railways, it is suggested that the copper tubing used could be $\frac{1}{8}$ in. or $\frac{5}{32}$ in. outside diameter and of fairly thin gauge, while the cylinders could be about $\frac{5}{16}$ in. diameter and about $\frac{3}{4}$ in. long, the pistons themselves being made at least $\frac{3}{8}$ in. long to ensure an air-tight fit; the pistons should be treated with graphite-grease on assembly.

A third method for operating both signals and points is an all-electric system using the commercial point "motors" for the pointwork, and individual solenoids for signals. As long as all the electrical gear is housed in weather-proof boxes alongside the track, the system is quite reliable. The point-motor should be covered by a box made up from brass sheet with soldered corners, this being arranged to completely cover both the motor and its base so that any rain cannot possibly get inside the mechanism. The signal box equipment will consist of small switches attached to the levers of a conventional lever frame or can be made up entirely of small tumbler or similar switches arranged on a panel. The current for operation of point motors and signal solenoids will generally be provided by a small car battery of either 6 or 12 volts according to the motors in use; the higher voltage is, however, always to be recommended.

The interlocking of lever frames is seldom attempted even on indoor model railways, but should not be ruled out, especially where most of the com-

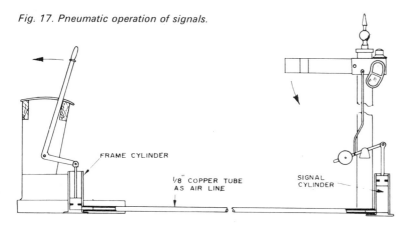

Fig. 17. Pneumatic operation of signals.

FRAME CYLINDER

1/8" COPPER TUBE
AS AIR LINE

SIGNAL
CYLINDER

plicated trackwork is inside a shed, as mentioned in an earlier chapter. If an interlocking lever frame is used in the open, it will need to be very thoroughly protected against the weather or it will be a constant source of trouble.

Telegraph poles are another item which are generally omitted on garden railways, as if they are made to anything like scale proportions, they are bound to be very flimsy and, in fact, if the wires between the poles were made to scale for a gauge "o" or gauge "1" railway, it is doubtful whether they would last for more than a few days if placed in the open.

Level crossings are other accessories which add to the scenic effects, although here again if they are to be made to work, the operating gear is somewhat complicated and in most cases the gates would be left permanently open for the benefit of the trains.

CHAPTER EIGHT

Locomotives and Electrification

Clockwork Locomotives

Nowadays, model railway enthusiasts tend to despise locomotives driven by clockwork, as they are generally unable to disassociate them from the toy tinplate sets of childhood days. It is true that over the last few years clockwork as a form of motive power for indoor railways has been almost entirely ousted by electric operation which gives a much greater amount of control over the trains.

On an outdoor model railway the length of run commanded by the average clockwork locomotive enables it to be operated to greater advantage. It can be used for terminus-to-terminus running, providing that the length of run does not exceed the spring capacity of the motor. Some quite good clockwork locomotives were made by the Trade up to 1939, most of the models made for gauge "0" and "1" being capable of covering about 120 ft. hauling a train of reasonable length.

Clockwork motors do not always receive the maintenance to which they are entitled. If they are cleaned and oiled regularly and never wound quite to the maximum capacity of the spring, they will give good service for many years. When operating them out of doors, they run better in fairly warm weather and in fact extremely cold weather is not too good for the spring.

The main difficulty in operating clockwork locomotives is to control them in a reasonable realistic manner. Starting is generally effected by releasing the brake on the engine by hand, but stopping often seems to entail grabbing the locomotive while in full flight which is clearly most un-railwaylike. Most clockwork motors are capable of being stopped and re-versed from the track though such devices are generally much too abrupt in their operation and can quite easily derail the rolling stock, particularly goods wagons.

A much better arrangement is to make up a braking-ramp consisting of a central rail up to about 2 ft. long which can be lifted at the end furthest away from the approaching engine. A shoe on the locomotive can then be made to engage with this ramp and be slightly lifted to apply brake shoes to the wheels. One advantage of this type of braking arrangement is that it can easily be worked in conjunction with the signals, so that the train can be stopped at the right point and then re-started when the ramp is lowered after the signal has been pulled off. See fig. 18.

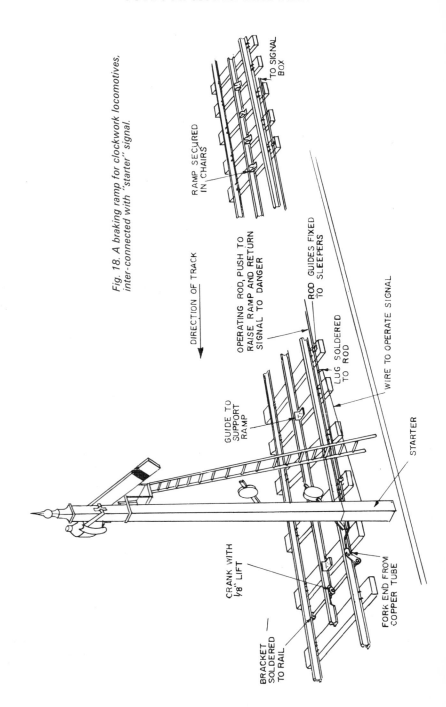

Fig. 18. A braking ramp for clockwork locomotives, inter-connected with "starter" signal.

DIRECTION OF TRACK

RAMP SECURED IN CHAIRS

TO SIGNAL BOX

OPERATING ROD, PUSH TO RAISE RAMP AND RETURN SIGNAL TO DANGER

ROD GUIDES FIXED TO SLEEPERS

LUG SOLDERED TO ROD

WIRE TO OPERATE SIGNAL

GUIDE TO SUPPORT RAMP

STARTER

CRANK WITH ⅛" LIFT

FORK END FROM COPPER TUBE

BRACKET SOLDERED TO RAIL

Steam Locomotives

Since the last war, the popularity of steam locomotives for gauge "o" seems to have steadily declined, but over the last two or three years there has been some revival, while the internally-fired steam locomotive for gauge "1" has become quite popular.

Like the clockwork engine, the model steam locomotive suffers from control difficulties and has several other disadvantages of its own, such as the time required to prepare it for operation, the messiness of working and the time involved in cleaning it down afterwards. On the other hand, all these disadvantages are completely outweighed by the fact that the model is propelled by the correct form of motive power. Apart from the obviously realistic appearance of the model steam locomotive hauling the trains, all the sounds characteristic of the steamer are present and, in fact, the whole operation is one of immense interest to the onlooker. The sharpening of the exhaust as the locomotive tackles a gradient, the smell of the hot oil, the clouds of steam, the odd dribbles of water on the track leave the operator in no doubt that he is dealing with a real railway locomotive with all the fascination of the full-size machine.

Model steam locomotives for gauge "o" and "1" can be divided into two main classes: (a) externally-fired low pressure locomotives, which are usually fitted with plain pot boilers, and (b) internally-fired high pressure engines.

Fig. 19 gives a general idea of the arrangement of an externally-fired steam locomotive for the smaller gauges. Although the boilers are generally of the plain pot variety, the water tube type is not entirely ruled out for the larger prototypes. Firing is generally by methylated spirit lamps which may be of the vaporising or wick type. The cylinders are normally fitted with pistons machined to an exact fit without any kind of packing, and this also applies to the valves which are generally of the simple piston type, so that the working efficiency of the whole engine depends very much on the lubricating system.

Fig. 19. General arrangement of an externally-fired model steam locomotive.

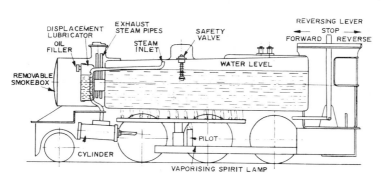

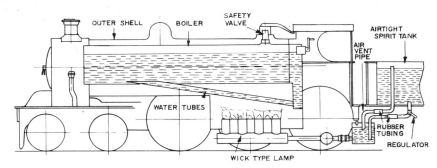

Fig. 20. General arrangement of an internally-fired model steam locomotive, with spirit firing.

The lubricators employed in these low pressure externally-fired models is nearly always of the displacement pattern, the oil container being located in the smokebox and taken down to the cylinders by the steam from the regulator. The lubricating oil used must be of a suitable heavy grade to ensure the steam-tightness of the pistons and valves. Such engines are very seldom fitted with superheaters and in fact superheating is generally unwise unless the pistons and valves are fitted with packing, which would be extremely difficult in such a small size.

Internally-fired high pressure steam locomotives are much to be preferred for working out of doors as they are unaffected by wind; the ordinary methylated spirit lamp generally used with the externally-fired low pressure model is only successful on a fairly calm day; as the flames from the burner are almost completely exposed, quite a moderate breeze is sufficient to put them out of action.

The most popular type of boiler for the small gauge internally-fired model is the water tube or Smithies type. In this a plain horizontal barrel is used, about two-thirds the diameter of the complete boiler and a number of water tubes are fitted beneath it shaped as shown in fig. 20. It is important that both the barrel and the tubes are made of seamless material, copper for preference, and that they are of fairly thin gauge. Firing may be by methylated spirit lamp, paraffin blowlamp or propane burner, the last mentioned being the most efficient and the most convenient.

Although not so often seen in the small gauges, the proper locomotive-type boiler can be recommended, but this need not necessarily be fired by solid fuel. If the tubes are made rather smaller in diameter than would be suitable for coal firing, such boilers are very effective with propane firing. Further details of steam locomotives in the smaller gauges can be obtained from the author's book "Model Locomotive Boilers, their Design and Construction".

Electric Locomotives

As was mentioned in Chapter One, electric operation is quite satisfactory

The author's "Firefly" seen on the track of the Chesterfield Model Engineering Society. The rails are of flat steel bar and the uprights are of brick construction.

A permanent outdoor track in 3½ in. gauge built in the form of a continuous concrete viaduct with flat bottom rails laid on wooden sleepers. The locomotive is J. H. Owen's Southern Railway Pacific "Hartland".

The track of the Hull Society during construction. Note the traverser running on rails at right angles to the main line.

On the Beech Hurst track of the Sussex Miniature Locomotive Society. Bill Carter is seen driving his famous "Atlantic" with K. N. Harris and G. W. Wildy as passengers.

A 5 in. gauge "Britannia" at work on a ground-level line in Australia.

A view on the track of the Witney Society at Blenheim Park. The track is laid on old full-size railway sleepers laid longitudinally. The author is seen at the controls of Mr. Bott's 4–6–4 tank locomotive.

in garden railways providing that certain rules are observed. The most important point is that the voltage used should be as high as possible. 6 to 8 volts is definitely too low, 12 volts is much better and, in fact, many successful electric garden railways employ this voltage, while 24 volts is probably the ideal from the electrical point of view. The main difficulty of using 24 volts is over the wiring of the electric motors used in the locomotives, as the great majority of the motors supplied by the Trade are wound for 12 volts.

There should be no difficulty in providing a suitable source of supply at 24 volts D.C. as this can be done by using two motor-car batteries coupled together in series. While these might sound rather expensive, it is not really essential to purchase new ones, as used batteries which are not quite up to the standard required for use in motor-cars, will still have some life left in them for the much lighter duty of powering a model railway.

Another source of supply is the combined transformer/rectifier and the ordinary commercial battery chargers giving 12 volts at 3 to 5 amps are quite effective.

Perhaps the most important decision to be taken when planning an electric garden railway is whether to adopt the two-rail system, the three-rail or the stud-contact system. The two-rail method of current collection involves insulating one running rail from the other and even if the contact between the wheels of the model and the rails is good, there is always the problem of leakage between the rails themselves, especially at pointwork and in wet weather. Generally speaking, therefore, the two-rail system should be ruled out in favour of one of the different types of three-rail pick-up.

At one time the most popular method of three-rail current collection was the outside third rail as used on the Southern Region. This is quite successful out of doors, providing that the third rail is kept absolutely clean, and the only real objection to its use is the somewhat unrealistic operation of steam-outline locomotives on electrified track.

In recent years, the stud-contact method of current collection has become quite popular, and in many ways this is ideal for outdoor railways as the rubbing action of the collector (usually described as the "skate") over the studs or pins automatically keeps these clean. The studs or pins used may be made of stainless steel, nickel-silver or brass, and even for the garden railway do not need to be larger in diameter than $\frac{1}{16}$ in., though for gauge "1" railways, something a little thicker is desirable.

As the studs do not need to be very much higher than the general level of the sleepers, except over pointwork, they are not at all obtrusive and, in fact, when the track has been properly ballasted, they will only be noticeable at very close quarters. Approaching points, the studs are raised carefully to a height about $\frac{1}{16}$ in. higher than the running rails and in garden railways it is most important that the studs should not be easily depressed through the weight of the locomotive pick-ups. To prevent this, a brass washer or collar a close fit on the stud can be soldered in position, so as to lie on top of the sleeper. This trouble can also be prevented if the electric wire used to wire up the studs underneath the track is of fairly heavy gauge, wrapped around each stud and soldered.

The collectors or "skates" used for the stud-contact system are generally of one or two main types, the "pantograph" type and the skate with a vertical guide and compression spring. Full details of how to make these current collectors are given in the author's "Miniature Locomotive Construction".

As mentioned earlier, with outdoor electric railways, it is not advisable to have too much complication in the open and this is where the layout which has a large terminus station sited in a shed or room of the house has much to commend it. Such layouts then require only the simplest electrical wiring out of doors.

It is sometimes claimed that if long stretches of electrified track are laid in the open, there will be a considerable voltage drop, unless additional heavy-gauge "feeders" are run out to points on the main line at intervals. While this may be beneficial where the track is of rather light construction, for instance the actual scale "o" gauge track, it should not be necessary with the standard "o" gauge or "1" gauge components, providing that all rail joints are separately wired up rather than relying on the friction grip of the fishplates.

One other system of electrification may be considered for an outdoor railway and this is the overhead wire system, the current collection being by pantographs as in the more recent examples of electrification on British Railways. This system would not, of course, be suitable for steam outline locomotives, but is very effective where the models in service are built to represent the modern electric locomotives.

Current collection with the overhead wire system is generally quite satisfactory but considerable maintenance may be required to ensure that the wires are properly supported, do not sag between their supports or get out of line in relation to the track. The actual wire used for the overhead system should be at least $\frac{1}{8}$ in. diameter or a square section may be preferred and it should be made of nickel-silver rather than brass for long life. Although copper may be better from the electrical conductivity point of view, it is really too soft for such a purpose and also stretches far too readily.

As regards the control and general wiring up of the outdoor electric line, while it is not essential to site all the controllers indoors, if they are arranged in the open they should be protected by boxes which are completely watertight, such boxes being made of metal with some form of rubber washer to ensure a good fit. The batteries or rectifiers supplying the whole railway must, of course, be kept indoors permanently and it should not be forgotten that even if the batteries are of large capacity and are only used at infrequent intervals, they must be given a regular charge at least once every ten days to ensure that they are kept in good condition.

CHAPTER NINE

Rolling Stock

IT MIGHT BE THOUGHT that the rolling stock for use on a garden railway can be exactly the same as on any normal indoor line. This is not, however, quite true as it will be found that die-cast wheels are more inclined to collect dirt when used in the open and it is, therefore, suggested that all rolling stock wheels should be of cast iron.

Generally speaking, model carriages and wagons used on outdoor lines do tend to receive rather rougher handling than those on the indoor railway, so it is suggested that they should be fairly strongly made and not fitted with quite so much fine detail; in any case, as the rolling stock in the garden is not usually seen at quite such close quarters as when indoors, a great deal of the fine detail work, brake gear, etc., would not be appreciated.

The bodies of both carriages and wagons should either be made in metal, plastic or wood, the last mentioned being quite satisfactory if given two or three coats of paint; cardboard construction should, however, be avoided as vehicles made entirely or partly of cardboard will not stand up to damp conditions for very long. Such parts as axle-boxes and coach bogie sides are better made of brass rather than the usual soft white metal, although this may limit somewhat the various types available from the Trade.

Painting of Locomotives

Model steam locomotives tend to get very wet and oily in use and frequent use of cotton waste or similar material is necessary to keep them reasonably clean. For this reason, too much external detail should not be added, especially to the running boards, and such things as lamp irons and other small details should be avoided as they tend to catch up in the material and become damaged or broken off altogether.

The paintwork of steam engines suffers a great deal from the heat, especially with external firing by methylated spirit lamp, so that wherever possible, stove-enamelling should be adopted. Most types of paint obtainable from the model trade are excellent when used on electrically-driven models, but are seldom suitable for stoving. A proper stove-enamel should, therefore, be obtained and the instructions of the paint manufacturers carefully followed. There are, of course, some stove-enamels which require a stoving temperature higher than the melting point of soft solder. Where soft solder has been used in the construction of the model, it will clearly not be possible to stove at anything like such a high temperature.

As regards such parts as the cylinders and smokeboxes of steam models, which are nearly always painted black on the prototype engine, a heat-resisting black enamel can be used, such as that obtainable from garages where it is used for finishing the exhaust systems of cars and motor-cycles.

For painting clockwork and electric locomotives and rolling stock, a good quality oil-based paint is suggested. The manufacturers' undercoat should be applied first, followed by three or four thin finishing coats. Where a proper paint spray apparatus is available, cellulose paints are to be preferred, but these paints are not recommended for hand brushing.

It is always false economy to purchase cheap paint brushes and either a sable or an ox-hair brush should be chosen for use with oil paints. For the average gauge "o" locomotive, a flat paint brush about ¾ in. wide is most suitable. The secret of obtaining a good finish with hand painting is undoubtedly careful preparation of the model in the first place and rubbing down with pumice powder in between each coat. Plenty of time should always be allowed between the application of each coat and it is well worthwhile waiting for a spell of dry weather for the best results.

When painting models of definite prototypes, care should be taken to get the exact shade of colour of the full-size locomotive. The "company" colours supplied by the model trade are generally quite accurate and if the builder has to mix his own paints, it is advisable to paint a fairly large piece of metal with the correct shade obtained from the model trader and use this for matching when mixing the paint. If the model is to be varnished after any lining or lettering has been applied, it will be found that the final colour will have altered considerably; this seems to apply particularly to Midland crimson lake or LMS maroon. This fact should be allowed for when mixing the primary colours.

Fig. 21. Layout of the track of the Birmingham S.M.E.

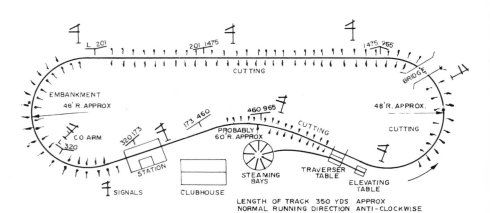

Many model locomotives and rolling stock are spoilt by bad lining and lettering. The author has often seen a magnificent model of some well-known full-size engine completely spoilt by incorrect lining or letters which are far too large or of the wrong shape. It should not be difficult to avoid this if the builder obtains a colour photograph or plate of the prototype, though even an ordinary black and white photograph will be found of some help. It is true that very few model enthusiasts can achieve neat lining and no amount of hints in this book will be of much help. Lining is something which can only be acquired by long practice on odd scraps of material, before the model itself is tackled.

Springing

It is surprising how few model constructors will go to the trouble of adding springing to their locomotives and rolling stock, but particularly on outdoor model railways, this refinement is well worth the additional trouble. Springing of wagons and coaches is not at all difficult and while that on locomotives makes for a certain amount of extra work, it should not be beyond the ability of the average model enthusiast. Details of locomotive springing are given in the author's book "Miniature Locomotive Construction".

CHAPTER TEN

Passenger-Carrying Railways

Raised Tracks

IN THE FIRST PART of this book, we dealt with scenic railways, which as we have seen are almost entirely of gauges "o" and "1", so we will now deal with those miniature railways in which the driver is hauled by the locomotive and, in fact, where quite large train loads of "live" passengers are hauled behind the engines.

It may be asked why scenic railways are so seldom built in the larger gauges such as $2\frac{1}{2}$ in. and $3\frac{1}{2}$ in. The answer really is that when we come to these bigger sizes, the locomotives are so powerful that it would not be safe to allow them to run on their own without a driver in constant attendance. In any case, most of the larger gauge steam locomotives built today are coal-fired and this would effectively rule out their use on scenic railways, short of a very elaborate system of automatic controls.

When dealing with railways carrying live passengers, the most important point to be decided at the outset is whether the track should be laid on the ground, or should be raised sufficiently above the ground to enable the driver and passengers to sit astride the passenger cars. Generally speaking, the carrying of passengers on ground level tracks should not be attempted on gauges less than 5 in. as even an acrobatic driver will have difficulty in keeping his balance on such a small gauge as $3\frac{1}{2}$ in. We may, therefore, say that raised tracks will be for railways of $2\frac{1}{2}$ in. to 5 in. gauge and ground level tracks will be those where the track gauge is $7\frac{1}{4}$ in. and above. Table I gives the popular track gauges in general use and also the approximate dimensions for the various gauges at the different scales. It will be noticed that in the U.S.A., models built to 1 in. scale (sometimes to 1/16 in. scale) use a track gauge of $4\frac{3}{4}$ in., while in the U.K., in South Africa, Australia and New Zealand and in one particular case in Canada, a gauge of 5 in. is used with a scale of 1 1/16 in. to the foot. Similarly, enthusiasts in the U.S.A. generally build their $1\frac{1}{2}$ in. scale models to run on a track gauge of $7\frac{1}{2}$ in., whereas the U.K. and Commonwealth countries almost universally use a gauge of $7\frac{1}{4}$ in. with this scale. This difference in track gauges is most unfortunate as it prevents the U.S.A. locomotive man ever having a run on a British line and vice versa. The author is at a loss to explain how this difference in gauge came about or, in fact, how the rather awkward scale of 1/16 in. to the foot originated.

46

As we have seen, raised tracks are normally used for $2\frac{1}{2}$ in., $3\frac{1}{2}$ in. and 5 in. gauge railways and these can be classified into two distinct types, a) portable tracks and b) permanent tracks.

TABLE I
Track Gauges, Scales and Loading Gauges.

Gauge	Scale	Loading Gauge
$2\frac{1}{2}$ in.	$\frac{17}{32}$ in. to ft.	$4\frac{3}{4}$ in. wide $\times 7\frac{1}{8}$ in. high
$3\frac{1}{2}$ in.	$\frac{3}{4}$ in. ,,	$6\frac{3}{4}$ in. $\times 10\frac{1}{8}$ in.
$4\frac{3}{4}$ in. (U.S.A.)	1 in. ,,	
5 in.	$1 \& \frac{1}{16}$ in. ,,	$9 \& \frac{9}{16}$ in. $\times 14\frac{3}{8}$ in.
$7\frac{1}{4}$ in.	$1\frac{1}{2}$ in. ,,	$13\frac{1}{2}$ in. $\times 20\frac{1}{4}$ in.
$7\frac{1}{2}$ in. (U.S.A.)	$1\frac{1}{2}$ in. ,,	
$9\frac{1}{2}$ in.	2 in. ,,	18 in. $\times 27$ in.
$10\frac{1}{4}$ in.	$2\frac{1}{4}$ in. ,,	$20\frac{1}{4}$ in. $\times 30\frac{1}{4}$ in.
15 in.	3 in. ,,	27 in. $\times 40\frac{1}{2}$ in.
15 in. (R.H.D.R. etc.)	4 in. ,,	36 in. $\times 54$ in.

TABLE II
Recommended Minimum Radii for Curves.

Gauge	Small tank engines, limited speed	Large engines, limited speed	Large engines, full speed
$2\frac{1}{2}$ in.	8 ft.	12 ft.	25 ft.
$3\frac{1}{2}$ in.	13 ft.	20 ft.	40 ft.
5 in.	16 ft.	25 ft.	50 ft.
$7\frac{1}{4}$ in.	25 ft.	50 ft.	100 ft.
$9\frac{1}{2}$ in.	30 ft.	60 ft.	120 ft.
$10\frac{1}{4}$ in.	40 ft.	80 ft.	160 ft.
15 in.	50 ft.	150 ft.	300 ft.

The above figures are only intended as general guidance. Clearly the exact radius which a locomotive will safely negotiate depends on many factors, such as fixed wheelbase, clearance between bogies and cylinders, etc. etc.

Portable Tracks

Many of the model engineering societies have built portable tracks either because of the lack of a suitable piece of land where a permanent track could be laid, or because they find such track most convenient when they are asked to run their railway in connection with a local fete and at similar public functions. Portable tracks are nearly always made of steel sections and figs. 21 and 22 show two popular forms of construction. A commonly made mistake is to use too thin a section of steel for the running rails, which is false economy, as not only will such a structure require a greater number of

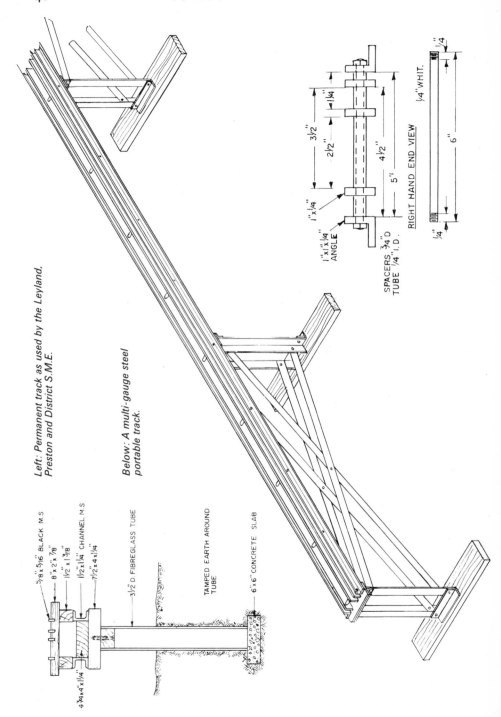

Left: Permanent track as used by the Leyland, Preston and District S.M.E.

Below: A multi-gauge steel portable track.

RIGHT HAND END VIEW

$\frac{1}{4}$" WHIT.

SPACERS, $\frac{3}{4}$" D.
TUBE $\frac{1}{4}$" I.D.

1" x 1" x $\frac{1}{4}$"
ANGLE

$\frac{5}{8}$" x $\frac{5}{16}$" BLACK M.S

8" x 2" x $\frac{7}{8}$"

$1\frac{1}{2}$" x $1\frac{3}{8}$"

$1\frac{1}{2}$" x $1\frac{1}{4}$" CHANNEL M.S

$7\frac{1}{2}$ x 4 x $1\frac{1}{4}$"

$3\frac{1}{2}$" D FIBREGLASS TUBE

TAMPED EARTH AROUND TUBE

6" x 6" CONCRETE SLAB

$4\frac{3}{4}$ x 4 x $1\frac{1}{4}$"

An outdoor line in New Brunswick, Canada, built with timber longitudinals and concrete uprights. The late Bob Baird with his 3½ in. gauge L.M.S. "Pacific".

A fine bridge on the narrow gauge 16.5 mm. track belonging to Mr. W. A. D. Strickland.

John Hurst of the Sydney Live Steamers and his 5 in. gauge 4–8–2 locomotive crossing a three-span steel girder bridge.

Passing through the cutting on the Guildford Society's track. Note the overbridge. (Photograph by the author.)

A picturesque station (Illshaw Heath) on the track of the Birmingham Society of Model Engineers. (Photograph— J. Balleny.)

A view on the track of the North London Society, showing Tytten- hanger station. Note the lamps and water columns. (Photograph— G. M. Cashmore.)

At a meeting of the New Jersey Live Steamers U.S.A., showing a 3½ in. gauge "Mogul" and a "Mallet".

A 5 in. gauge LMS 4–6–0 Jubilee class locomotive on the permanent track of the Rugby Society, which uses steel flats for rails with concrete viaduct foundation. (Photograph by the author.)

A meeting of the South Australia Society of Model and Experimental Engineers, showing permanent tracks for $2\frac{1}{2}$ in., $3\frac{1}{2}$ in. and 5 in. gauges and boating pond.

A picture taken on the old ground-level track of the Derby Society of Model Engineers, showing locomotive sidings.

Another view of the permanent track of the Rugby Society, showing concrete uprights with wooden blocks for adjustment. (Photograph by the author.)

supporting uprights, but the narrow railhead causes loss of adhesion for the locomotive driving wheels.

Portable tracks where the rails are composed of flat steel laid on edge should stand up to British weather conditions quite successfully, provided that they are properly galvanised and then given at least two coats of good quality paint after final assembly. The sections of a portable track should not be made too long, as it must not be forgotten that they will have to be loaded on and off lorries or the owner's shooting-brake or similar vehicle and particular care should be given to the form of coupling to be used between each section. It is a good plan to number each section and each rail joint so that the sections are always assembled in the same order. In this form of track, one single gauge is obviously out of the question and, in fact, an attempt should be made to accommodate as many gauges as possible in the rail assembly so that visitors to the Rally will be able to run their locomotives whatever gauge these happen to be.

It should not be forgotten that as a portable track may have to be set up in a field where the surface may be anything but dead level and smooth; the feet of the uprights should be made as wide as possible and of such a design that they can be levelled without much difficulty.

While a portable track can be made almost entirely from wood, using wooden sleepers laid at approximately scale spacing and proper rail section held down to the sleepers by brass wood screws and clips, such a track tends to get out of line much more easily than the all-steel track referred to previously. Fig. 23 shows one construction which has been used by one of our model engineering societies with reasonable success, but the all-steel portable track is to be recommended.

Permanent Raised Tracks

There are many different methods of making a permanent raised track, the basic forms of construction being a wooden framework, an all-steel framework or a reinforced concrete structure, or a combination of any of these three. It is important to decide the minimum height of a raised track above the level of the ground and it is suggested that this should be at least 16 in. to allow sufficient room for the driver's and passengers' legs. At the same time it should not be forgotten that the higher the rails are from the ground, the greater the possibility of damage which might arise from an accident. A careless or inexperienced passenger or even the driver himself may lose his balance and sometimes even the engine itself may de-rail, and the further it falls the longer it is going to be in the sheds for repairs. Of course, where the land on which the railway is sited is very uneven, it may be impossible to avoid some sections of track being rather high from ground level, but wherever possible the height of the raised track should not be more than 2 ft. to 2 ft. 6 in.

If the permanent track is being built in the owner's own garden, he may decide to limit it to the one particular rail gauge in which he is interested.

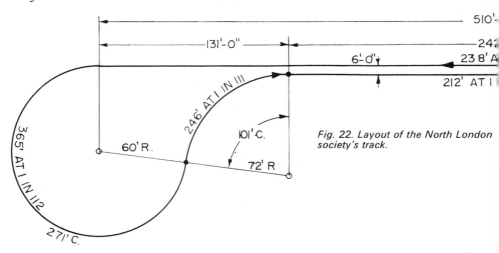

Fig. 22. Layout of the North London society's track.

But even on such a railway, it is highly desirable to be able to accommodate "foreign" locomotives of other gauges, and as it is very difficult to add additional rails to a finished track, it is suggested that a multi-gauge track should be seriously considered at the outset.

There is an additional point that if the owner's locomotives are all for 3½ in. gauge, an additional rail can still be added to enable the passenger cars to run on a 5 in. gauge track, which will give a much more stable car and lessen the possibility of accidents due to loss of balance. It is quite possible to arrange four running rails so that the track can be used for all three of the popular gauges—2½ in., 3½ in. and 5 in.; such a track may not only be a great source of pleasure to its owner, but also one to which he can invite owners of locomotives of gauges other than his own.

Builders of outdoor passenger-carrying tracks are often puzzled over the choice between adopting rails made from ordinary flat steel bar or steel angle or a proper railway track using the correct flat-bottomed rail and wooden sleepers more or less to scale proportions. At the present time, it is difficult to obtain a proper model rail section in steel or brass, but such a section is readily available in an aluminium alloy.

It is generally agreed that the aluminium alloy track gives a smooth ride and at least on the smaller gauges (2½ to 3½ in.) the adhesion of the driving wheels of the locomotive is adequate. When this alloy rail is adopted for 5 in. and 7¼ in. gauge, however, the width of the railhead is not really adequate to give good adhesion for the wheels. As far as appearance goes, the proper rail section with wooden sleepers is, of course, much more realistic.

Wooden Construction

If a wooden superstructure is decided upon, the uprights should be of a section at least 4 in. × 4 in. and these should be arranged at intervals of not more than 5 ft., allowing at least 1 ft. of the height of the uprights to be set

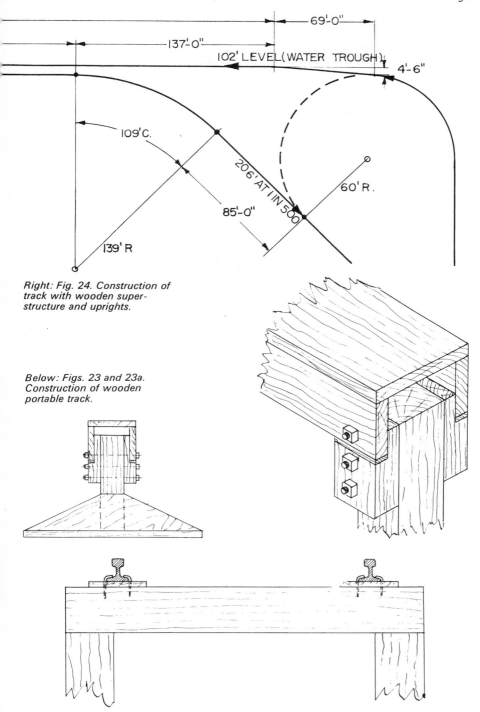

69'-0"

137'-0"

102' LEVEL (WATER TROUGH)

4'-6"

109'C.

206' AT I IN 500

60'R.

85'-0"

139' R

Right: Fig. 24. Construction of track with wooden super-structure and uprights.

Below: Figs. 23 and 23a. Construction of wooden portable track.

into the ground. The uprights may either be put direct into the earth after
thoroughly soaking in creosote or they may be put into holes of about three
times the size of the posts, these holes being then filled with concrete. It is
not, however, definitely established whether the wooden post set into
concrete lasts very much longer than those put direct into the earth. See
fig. 3.

The longitudinal planks, which will be 5 ft. long, should be of a section at
least 6 in. × 1 in., and if these are arranged with an insert of 4 × 2 section and
bolted right through as shown in fig. 24, a ready means of adjusting the height
of the track will be achieved.

Metal Construction

Not many permanent tracks have been built using an all-metal construction. This is probably because such tracks would have to be built almost
entirely of steel for reasons of economy, and however carefully the steel
sections are galvanised or painted (or both), rust seems to set in sooner or
later. Light alloy sections might be worth considering for the supports,
especially those parts of the uprights which have to be put into the ground,
and a useful track can be constructed in this way as shown in fig. 25. One
possible disadvantage of the all-metal track is that it tends to be rather noisy
and gives rather a hard ride.

Below and R.H. page. Fig. 25. Construction of an all-metal permanent track.

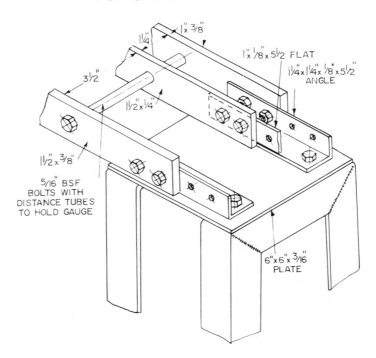

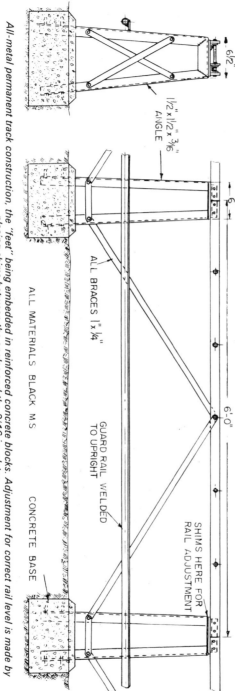

6½"

1½" x 1½" x 3/16"
ANGLE

6"

ALL BRACES 1" x ¼"

GUARD RAIL WELDED
TO UPRIGHT

6'-0"

SHIMS HERE FOR
RAIL ADJUSTMENT

ALL MATERIALS BLACK M S   CONCRETE BASE

All-metal permanent track construction, the "feet" being embedded in reinforced concrete blocks. Adjustment for correct rail level is made by placing shims between the angles and the 3/16 in. plates.

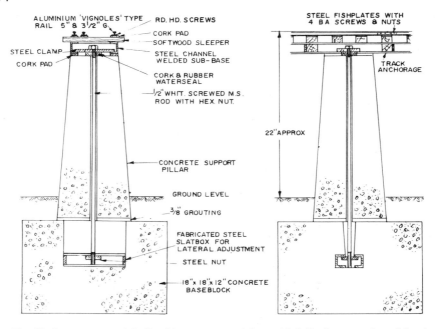

Fig. 26. Permanent track built with concrete uprights, with full adjustment for rail level.

Brick and Concrete Construction

Some permanent tracks have been built using uprights constructed with bricks and with wooden longitudinal sections in between the uprights. Reinforced concrete is, however, undoubtedly the most satisfactory and long-lasting of all the various types. Sometimes the uprights only are built in reinforced concrete, the longitudinals being of wood or metal, while occasionally the whole structure is made in the form of pre-cast units which may be cast in suitable boxes or cast on the site by the aid of "shuttering".

The important thing to remember with concrete uprights is to provide for vertical adjustment of the longitudinals so as to allow for any slight sinking of the uprights. Several methods for providing this adjustment are shown in Fig. 26. Those who prefer a wooden construction for the longitudinals might consider the use of old railway sleepers, which can generally be obtained from British Railways at a moderate figure.

Rails for Permanent Tracks

As with the portable track, the choice of suitable rail is generally between flat steel bar laid on edge and the correct rail section made in light alloy.

As mentioned previously, it may be difficult to obtain the correct rail section in either steel or brass—the latter material is, in any case, liable to prove very expensive in the section suitable for $3\frac{1}{2}$ in. or 5 in. gauges. If flat steel bar is adopted, this should, if possible, be galvanised before use and given two good coats of bituminous paint *after* final assembly, which will keep rust at bay for at least a reasonable time.

For 2½ in. or 3½ in. gauge railways, steel bar about 1 in. × ¼ in. laid on edge is satisfactory, but for 5 in. gauge the bar used should be ⅜ in. thick, to provide good adhesion for the locomotives.

Fig. 26a. Another method of construction for permanent tracks, as used by the North London Society of Model Engineers.

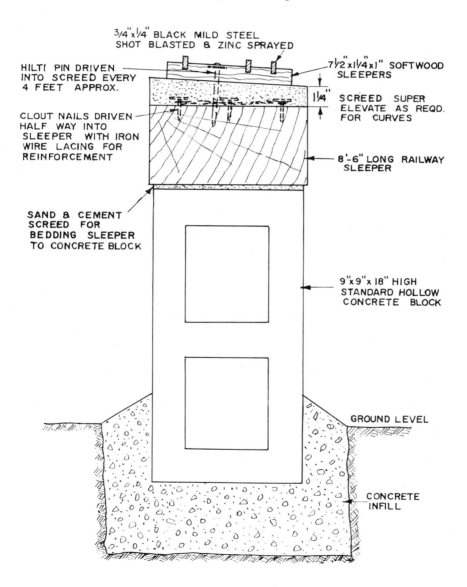

The flat-bottomed rail is sometimes spiked direct to the wooden sleepers, using dog-spikes, while one occasionally sees ordinary brass wood screws put in on each side of the rail at a slight angle, with brass washers under the screwheads engaging the base of the rail. But a much sounder method is to cut proper rail-plates from brass or light alloy strip, or from galvanised or sheradised steel. These are drilled for the screws and brass roundhead screws about $\frac{3}{4}$ in. long (according to the thickness of the sleepers) screwed home, one on each side of the rail.

There are several ways of securing rails made of flat steel bar to the sleepers. One method consists of milling out the sleeper itself to a depth equal to about half the depth of the rail, i.e. $\frac{3}{8}$ in. for a rail made from steel bar $\frac{3}{4}$ in. $\times \frac{1}{4}$ or $\frac{3}{8}$ in. thick. The slots must of course be cut at the exact distance apart so as to maintain the correct rail gauge, not forgetting that if the railway contains some sharp curves, a slight increase in gauge may be necessary.

Another method is to first bolt the two or more rails to one another by means of steel rod threaded at each end, with steel tube cut to the required length to suit the gauge or gauges of the track to act as spacers. The track is then held down by clamps over the spacing tubes at reasonable intervals.

A third method, and perhaps the best of the three, is to weld the rails to steel "rail-plates", which are drilled to take wood screws, one on each side of each rail. For a 5 in. gauge track, using wooden sleepers say 1 in. $\times \frac{3}{4}$ in. section, the rail-plates may be about $\frac{3}{4}$ in. wide $\times$ 1$\frac{1}{4}$ in. long $\times \frac{1}{8}$ in. thick. After laying, such a track should be given two good coats of a bituminous paint. This makes a good track, and is one that will not need much maintenance except in very wet climates. When adjustment is required, the rail-plates may be shifted without much difficulty.

Sleepers

Sleepers for permanent outdoor passenger-carrying tracks should be made of sound wood; while teak is the most durable, it is far too hard for easy working and is expensive. Other woods worth considering are oak (still hard to work) and good-quality soft woods such as cedar or pine. The sleepers should be planed on all sides and after cutting to length (for which a simple jig should be made), they should be soaked in a strong solution of creosote or a good proprietary wood preservative overnight before commencing track laying. Suggested sleeper sizes for the various gauges are given in table III.

Table III

Recommended Sleeper Sizes

For Raised Tracks

2$\frac{1}{2}$ in. gauge	5 in. long $\times \frac{3}{4}$ in. $\times \frac{3}{4}$ in.
3$\frac{1}{2}$ in. gauge	6 in. long $\times \frac{3}{4}$ in. $\times \frac{3}{4}$ in.
5 in. gauge	7$\frac{3}{4}$ in. long $\times$ 1 in. $\times \frac{3}{4}$ in.
7$\frac{1}{4}$ in. gauge	10 in. long $\times$ 1$\frac{1}{2}$ in. $\times$ 1 in.

A heavy load of young passengers seen on the old track of the Chingford & District Society. The locomotive is the club's Atlantic "Firefly". (Photograph—C. B. Capener.)

A view of Mr. Harper's old track at Bromley, showing 2–10–0 locomotive on the turntable. A King Arthur class 4–6–0 is seen on the right, and passenger truck on the left. (Photograph by the author.)

Group Capt. Law raising steam on a 5 in. gauge 2–10–0 locomotive at Mr. Harper's track at Bromley, Kent (now dismantled.)   (Photograph by the author.)

A pivoted bridge or traverser on a 5 in. gauge outdoor railway, constructed mainly of steel tubing.

A fine concrete bridge on Mr. Harper's old track at Bromley, Kent. (Photograph by the author.)

Seen on the North London Society's track; "breather" switches to allow for expansion, fitted at regular intervals of approximately 160 ft. The direction of travel in the picture is left to right. (Photograph—G. M. Cashmore.)

For Ground Level Tracks

3½ in. gauge	7½ in. long × ¾ in. × ¾ in.
5 in. gauge	10 in. long × 1 in. × ¾ in.
7¼ in. gauge	14 in. long × 1½ or 1¾ in. × 1 in.
9½ in. gauge	18 in. long × 1¾ or 2 in. × 1 or 1¼ in.
10¼ in. gauge	20 in. long × 2 or 2¼ in. × 1¼ or 1½ in.
15 in. gauge	29 in. long × 3 in. × 2 in.

Recommended Sleeper Spacing
(Centre-to-centre)

2½ in. gauge	2¼ in.	3½ in. gauge	2¼ in.
5 in. gauge	3 in.	7¼ in. gauge	4½ to 5 in.
9½ in. gauge	6 in.	10¼ in. gauge	6½ in.
15 in. gauge	9 in.		

It will be noted from these tables that sleepers for raised tracks do not need to be so long as for those used on ground level tracks, which are dependent for their alignment on good ballasting. A point worth noting is that on raised tracks, the ends of the sleepers should not be allowed to project beyond the longitudinals beneath them (a common fault) or at least a longitudinal strip should be fitted along the ends of the sleepers to prevent anything from the train catching them and causing an accident.

When screwing the sleepers down to the longitudinals (for which brass galvanised or plated screws should be used), care should be taken to ensure that their heads do not get in the way of the dog-spikes or rail-plate screws used for holding down the rails.

Where the longitudinal members of a permanent track are in the form of reinforced concrete units, if the tops of these are made reasonably smooth and level, it is possible to cement the wooden sleepers direct to the concrete, for which purpose a special cement has been developed.

Such a construction has recently been adopted by the Bournemouth Society of Model Engineers for their new continuous track.

Rail Joints

When using aluminium alloy rails, or in fact any rails of correct shape, whether bullhead or flat-bottomed, proper fishplates should be used, bolted to the rail ends as in full-size practice, using plated screws, and not forgetting to allow a small expansion gap if the track is being laid in any but very hot weather.

The question of allowing for expansion when using flat steel bar for rails is a very debatable one. Some builders have achieved success by welding all the rail ends together, thus producing in effect one long length of rail. In such a case, the expansion of the metal in hot weather appears to be absorbed in the material itself; but if such a rail is welded to steel rail-plates, and these are screwed to the sleepers, it is not difficult to arrange for some small longitudinal movement between the track and the bed.

Layout of the Track

The layout of a permanent railway track will clearly depend on the shape and size of the ground available, and if there is any choice in the matter, a reasonably flat piece of land should be chosen. Although a continuous track is obviously desirable, this need not necessarily prove uninteresting, as there are many ways of arranging the layout other than a straightforward oval. Some Club tracks have in fact been built on more than one level, one track crossing over the other on a suitable bridge or viaduct.

The first thing to do before designing any trackwork is to make a scale plan of the site, to as large a scale as possible, showing the boundaries, hedges, trees, gates, etc, noting any obstructions that cannot be removed, so that the track may be planned to by-pass them with adequate clearance. In the case of the larger club and society tracks, it is often found that one of the members is a trained surveyor, or one of the members has a friend with the required knowledge who can be persuaded to help in surveying the area and taking the levels, but for the benefit of the individual with no such knowledge, the following suggestions are made. Do not rush out and buy an expensive theodolite. The only really essential equipment is a good tape measure, strong cord, of a type which will not shrink or stretch appreciably (or alternately—steel wire) a spirit level 12 in. or 18 in. size, and suitable stakes. Tape measures are made in 25 ft., 33 ft., 50 ft., 66 ft. and 100 ft. lengths, and can be obtained in linen, steel, metallic with copper reinforcing, or plastic-coated metal varieties. All these types, with the exception of linen, can be used.

If the site is at all irregular in shape, the first thing to do is to choose the longest side, and just inside this, lay a cord between two stakes, one at each end, as shown in Fig. 27. From this base-line, AB in the illustration, the location of any trees or bushes, and the position of all of the boundaries of the site can be laid off by means of "offsets".

Fig. 27. Surveying the site for the track layout.

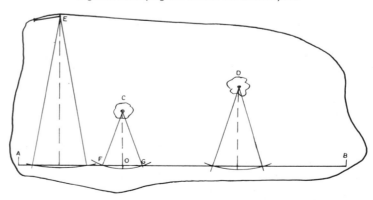

For instance, in Fig. 27 suppose AB is the base-line, and C and D are trees and E a gate post, the exact location of which are required. To take tree C first, a cord somewhat longer than is required to reach to the base-line is attached to the tree and then stretched across the base-line at F. A stake is then put in at F and a knot or other mark put on the cord at the same point. The cord is now swung in an arc, cutting the base-line again at G, where another stake is put in the ground. It is now a simple matter to measure the distances AF and AG, mark them off on the scale plan, and strike arcs from centres F and G to find the exact position of C. The exact positions of E and D can be found in relation to the base-line in a similar manner.

It may be asked, why not simply take the cord from (say) C at right angles to the base-line, and measure the offset directly. The difficulty with this method is that in the field, it is not easy to be sure when the cord is exactly at right angles, unless a very large square is available.

The levels of the site may be taken as shown in Fig. 28, a method which is sufficiently accurate for a small layout. Sometimes it happens that a tree or other obstruction blocks the line of sight. In this case, it becomes necessary to transfer a level from one point to another until all parts of the site have been covered.

Another method of obtaining the levels on a small site is by the use of an "Aqualev". This consists of a long length of rubber or plastic tube attached at each end to glass tubes containing floats. The tubes are attached to vertical posts or stands and the measurements are then taken from the appropriate mark on the float to the ground. As the glass tubes are inter-connected with the rubber tubing and the whole filled with water, the floats will of course come to rest at exactly the same level.

A simple "Aqualev" can be made from two lengths of glass tube attached to suitable wooden stands, and the garden hose used to connect the two. Care should be taken to ensure that the glass tubes are held truly vertical; this can be checked by a plumb bob and line.

Where the site causes a considerable fluctuation in the level of the track itself, some economy in the uprights can be obtained by incorporating suitable inclines; these will, in any case, add considerably to the interest of driving the locomotives, but they should not be made too severe, otherwise the smaller and less powerful engines will be at a serious disadvantage. A gradient of about 1 in 60 should be regarded as about the steepest for the average track, though even this may be on the severe side for tracks on which heavy passenger loads are to be hauled. For the average club track, a maximum incline of about 1 in 100 is suggested.

Sidings and Turntables

It is most important, especially when designing Club tracks, that adequate provision be made for locomotive sidings or steaming bays. Two types of steaming bay seem to be in general use. One consists of the installation of a turntable on the main line, with sidings laid out at various angles to the

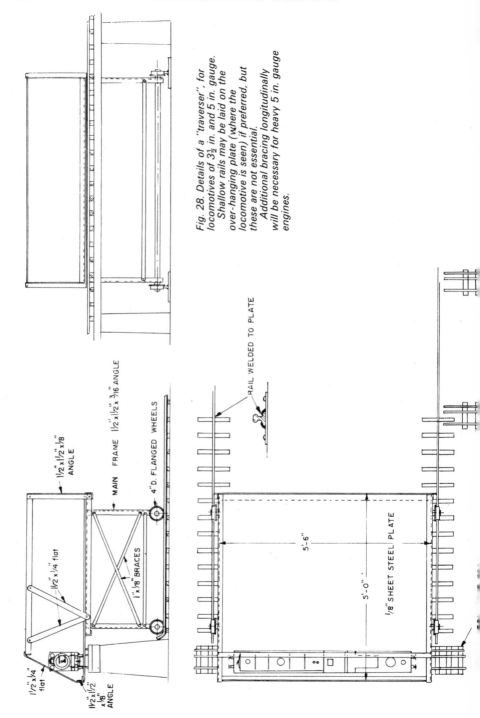

Fig. 28. Details of a "traverser", for locomotives of 3½ in. and 5 in. gauge. Shallow rails may be laid on the over-hanging plate (where the locomotive is seen) if preferred, but these are not essential.
Additional bracing longitudinally will be necessary for heavy 5 in. gauge engines.

RAIL WELDED TO PLATE

MAIN FRAME 1½" x 1½" x ³⁄₁₆" ANGLE

4" D. FLANGED WHEELS

1½" x 1½" x ⅛" ANGLE

½" x ¼" flat

½" x ¼" flat

1 x ⅛" BRACES

½" x ¼" flat

1½" x 1½" x ⅛" ANGLE

5'-6"

5'-0"

⅛" SHEET STEEL PLATE

main line, so that engines can quickly run out on to the turntable and thence on to the main line. This system is not however recommended as it means that the traffic on the main line has to be brought to a halt every time an engine has to be shunted from one siding to another. Another disadvantage of this system is the difficulty in getting the rails on the turntable to line up accurately with the rails on the main line. This is not difficult when the turntable is first built and erected, but trouble arises later on, in service, due to the ravages of the climate. Some form of locking device should always be incorporated in a turntable situated on a main line. It is also essential to protect the turntable by colour-light signal or semaphore signal, interlocked with the turntable, so that if the turntable is not exactly lined up, the signals protecting it are held at danger.

Sometimes the turntable is not of the conventional type with centre pivot. The pivot may be placed at one end, the outer end being supported by wheels which run on a stretch of flat concrete laid at the appropriate radius, so that the wheels cannot run off into soft ground and upset the alignment of the track.

Another, and better, method of enabling locomotives to be prepared for running without interfering with those already on the main line is the traverser. This should be of substantial construction and preferably long enough to accommodate the longest locomotive likely to run on the track, plus one passenger car. The traverser is fitted with flanged wheels, which run on rails laid at right-angles to the main line.

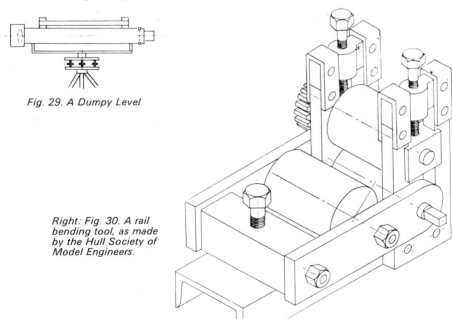

Fig. 29. A Dumpy Level

Right: Fig. 30. A rail bending tool, as made by the Hull Society of Model Engineers.

It is not essential that the rails on the traverser should actually form parts of the track of the main line when in position, as this would prevent its use for transferring engines from one siding to another without leaving a big gap in the main line. A better method is to make the main line continuous, with no gap at all, and arrange the traverser so that the rails on it are just high enough to clear the rails of the main line. When it is required to move a locomotive from the traverser to the main line, the traverser is moved so that its track lies immediately over the main line, it being arranged with sufficient overhang to allow for this. It is then a simple matter to move the locomotive forward over the ends of the rails on the traverser on to the rails of the main line, after which the traverser is immediately moved back out of the way, to line up with one of the sidings. See Fig. 28.

CHAPTER ELEVEN

Ground Level Tracks

IT IS SOMETIMES ASKED whether it is possible to have a miniature railway as small as $3\frac{1}{2}$ in. gauge laid direct on the ground. While this is quite feasible if an extra rail is laid to a larger gauge, say 5 in., on which the passenger cars could run; to expect passengers to balance on cars running on $3\frac{1}{2}$ in. gauge would be almost asking for acrobats! Even a 5 in. gauge ground level railway needs a great deal of care in operation, though there is the advantage that if either the locomotive or the passengers cars or contents DO come off the track, they do not have very far to fall!

But a 5 in. ground level railway, or a combined $3\frac{1}{2}$ in./5 in. line can be most interesting to operate, as anyone who has seen the railway operated by the Derby Society of Model Engineers can testify.

Perhaps it is on $7\frac{1}{4}$ in. gauge that the ground level line really comes into its own, and there are quite a large number of such miniature railways now operating successfully, both in this country and abroad. (In North America, the gauge usually adopted is $7\frac{1}{2}$ in., rather than $7\frac{1}{4}$ in.). Undoubtedly the greatest attraction of this type of line is the fact that points and crossings can be introduced and scenic attractions such as tunnels and bridges can be built more easily, adding greatly to the interest of operation and maintenance.

It is sometimes imagined that the laying of the ground level line is very much easier than a raised track. This is not necessarily so, however, though it depends very much on the nature of the ground. In fact, it is seldom possible to lay the track directly on the earth. As the question of drainage, as well as the proper supporting of the weight of the rolling stock and passengers have to be considered, the line must be properly ballasted, as on the full-size railway. The basic construction of such a track is as shown in Fig. 31 where it will be seen that the ballast is graded so as to provide coarser material at the bottom and a finer ballast underneath and around the sleepers.

The sleepers themselves should be fairly substantial, as they have to carry a greatly "out-of-scale" weight, and as a rough guide, their length should be at least twice the gauge of the rails. The width and depth of the sleepers should be approximately 20 per cent greater than the scale size of the prototype (the standard British Rail sleeper is 8 ft. 6 in. long × 10 in. × 5 in.) and the spacing should be such that the distance between any two sleepers is not greater than three times the width of the sleepers. At rail joints, the sleepers may be placed a little closer than the foregoing.

The laying of a ground level track basically follows full-size practice in that after the track has been prepared, the sleepers are set into the ballast and lined up in both planes before the rails are laid. A large spirit level, suitable wooden pegs and wire of sufficiently heavy section to eliminate stretching, will be found most useful for lining up the sleepers.

The laying of a ground level track basically follows full-size practice in that after the track has been prepared, the sleepers are set into the ballast and lined up in both planes before the rails are laid. A large spirit level, suitable wooden pegs and wire of sufficiently heavy section to eliminate stretching, will be found most useful for lining up the sleepers.

Proper flat-bottomed steel rail and suitable dog spikes for the larger gauges (9½ in. upwards) can generally be obtained from firms who specialise in the manufacture of track and materials for the narrow gauges and contractors' railways. These companies usually supply suitable fishplates, point levers and other accessories.

After the rails have been laid on the sleepers, lined up and spiked down, the spirit level is used to check that the rails are level on each side; the exact alignment of the sleepers is then effected by "tamping"—i.e., by jacking up the end of the sleeper which is too low and raking in further ballast until the level has been corrected. A suitable trolley carrying plenty of weight is then run slowly over the track, allowing it to settle, when it is again checked and tamping carried out if necessary. Further settlement will of course take place over a period of time, so that correction may be necessary from time to time in the course of normal maintenance.

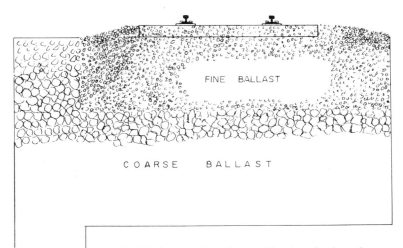

FINE   BALLAST

COARSE   BALLAST

Fig. 31. Construction of ground level track where the ground is damp or boggy.

A lattice girder bridge supported on stone abutments on Mr. Harper's track at Bromley. (Photograph by the author.)

Another picture taken on the North London Society's track. The rail joints are brazed together using $\frac{1}{2}$ in. channel section 3 in. long. After brazing the joint is zinc painted. The picture shows a joint before painting. (Photograph—G. M. Cashmore.)

Level crossing gate and garden shed on Mr. Harper's old railway at Bromley. (Photograph by the author.)

This picture shows the construction of the track built by the Urmston Society. The concrete pillars are 15 in. high with a 12 in. square base, tapering towards the top.

Further work on the North London extension. Note wire reinforcements before cementing. (Photograph— G. M. Cashmore.)

A steel tube is put through the centre so that a 'J' bolt can be placed through to bolt the channel to the pillar.

The author driving on the new track of the Bournemouth Society of Model Engineers. This picture was taken in heavy rain.

Work in progress on the new extension of the North London Society's track. Shutter boards are placed at each side of the supporting sleepers and nailed in position. The nail heads are left proud for easy removal of boards after cementing. Left—Ron Price, right— Mike Crisp. (Photograph—G. M. Cashmore.)

A section of the main line on the North London Society's track at Colney Heath, showing the construction. (Photograph by G. M. Cashmore.)

This photograph was taken after the rebuilding of the track of the Chingford and District Society, and shows the unusual bridge.

A fine multiple gauge outdoor railway, showing a brick-built overbridge.

Part of the track of the Guildford Society, showing concrete uprights and steel rail construction. (Photograph by the author.)

North London S.M.E. A special saw bench was made for slotting the sleepers to take the rails to suit $3\frac{1}{2}$ in. and 5 in. gauges. Twelve sleepers are slotted in one operation. (Saw and photograph by G. M. Cashmore.)

The unusual double-swing gates allowing access to the centre of the track on the layout of the Guildford Model Society. Note the concrete laid in a quarter circle for the wheel supporting the bridge spans to work upon. (Photograph by the author.)

Another view of the Guildford Society's track, showing traverser, locomotive sidings and water tower. (Photograph by the author.)

A fine tunnel mouth built by members of the North London Society of Model Engineers. Note gradient post and colour light signal. (Photograph—G. M. Cashmore.)

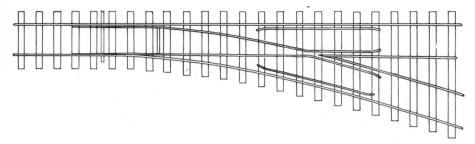

Fig. 32. Details of a right-hand turnout.

Pointwork

When constructing points for gauges of 3½ in. upwards, whether flat-bottomed rail or flat steel bar is used, it should be noted that some form of slide chair will be required, to support the ends of the point blades. Sometimes the flat steel used for rails is let into the sleepers, the sleepers being milled out in a jig to receive them at the correct distance apart; in such a case, the sleepers carrying the point blades may be set lower in the ballast, so that lengths of steel plate or strip can be inserted underneath the stock rail, to which it may be welded, the strip being screwed down to the sleeper at each end.

In the construction of points for the larger gauges, full-size design may be followed very closely, the moving blades being fishplated to the closing rails, which again may be fishplated to the crossing rails or "frog", so that the latter component may be made up as a separate unit. The frog, wing rails and check rails may all be welded to steel strips or plates laid underneath the rails on top of the sleepers, the sleepers carrying these parts being set slightly lower in the ballast as at the blade end of the turnout.

Switches may be made with either straight or curved crossings, but the difference is not greatly noticeable in the smaller gauges. In any case, switches which are taken at speed on the main line should always be arranged "trailing", rather than "facing".

In full-size practice, switches on main lines vary in angle from 1 in 8 to 1 in 20, while in sidings, angles as large as 1 in 4 may be found. For a 5 in. gauge railway, a crossing angle of 1 in 8 will give very smooth running. This corresponds to a radius on the switch rails of about 52 ft.

Super-elevation

Super-elevation on curved track should not be neglected, even on a ground level line. Apart from the greater safety obtained, riding will be found more comfortable.

The amount of super-elevation required may be calculated from the following formula:–

$$\text{S.E.} = \frac{G \times V^2}{R \times 40} \text{ (inches)}$$

Where G is the rail gauge in inches.

V is the average maximum speed of the train in miles per hour.

R is the radius of the curved track in feet.

As an example of the working of this formula, suppose the train is working on 5 in. gauge track with a maximum speed of 10 m.p.h. and the radius of the track is 50 ft. Then the required super-elevation would be 1/4 in. It should be noted that this dimension refers to the height of the outside rail above the inside rail, NOT to the amount the outer ends of the sleepers should be raised. This would be about double the above figure, according to the length of the sleepers.

The above formula does not give the theoretically correct amount of super-elevation, but somewhat less. However the modern tendency is to allow rather less than formerly, as it has been found in practice that super-elevation can be reduced safely and without discomfort. It is important that the amount of super-elevation selected is attained from the level gradually.

On ground level lines, the super-elevation can generally be achieved by carefully tamping of the ballast, no alteration being made to the sleepers themselves.

Transition curves

It is suggested that on all tracks above $2\frac{1}{2}$ in. gauge, some form of transition curve, or "easement spiral", is worth considering. In full-size practice, the cubic parabola is generally used and is set out by means of rectangular offsets from the tangent. Transition curves form rather a problem in small scale work, but the following method is suggested for tracks of gauges from $3\frac{1}{2}$ in. to $7\frac{1}{4}$ in.

Suppose the curve concerned is to be a quarter circle—very common in small gauge work—then start by marking out a normal quarter circle to the required radius, with centre A (Fig. 33) and radius AB. Draw AC at right angles to AB, AC of course being equal to AB. Then join CB and mark a point D one third of the length CB from C. In other words CD equals one third CB. Now draw AE through D, AE being equal to AB. Then the arc EB will form the normal radius R, while the arc EC is to be abandoned in favour of the transition curve OE. The transition curve is established as follows :–

It will be noted that obtaining a transition curve by this method, one has to work backwards from the final or normal radius, but this is not thought to be any disadvantage in practice, as the track can be drawn out on the drawing board first, to as large a scale as possible, so that the approximate position of O can be determined before starting work in the field.

It will also be noted that the whole of the field work çan be done by trammels, cord, or wire. For large radii, wire is to preferred, and this should be heavy enough to eliminate stretching as far as possible. Trees and other obstructions certainly make the laying out of such a transition curve very difficult, but once the various centres are established and "pegged", the curves may be laid out as far as the obstruction, the wire then brought to the other side of the obstruction, and the curve completed.

As an example of the above method, suppose the normal radius of the curve is to be 50 ft. Then the first arc OH will be 100 ft. radius, the second arc HG will be 80 ft. radius, the third arc GF will be 65 ft. radius, and the fourth arc FE will be 55 ft. radius. From E onwards of course, the radius will be the normal one of 50 ft.

The lengths of the arcs will be approximately as follows:– HG—7·14 ft., GF—5·55 ft., FE—4·55 ft. Arc OH will be a little under 10 ft.

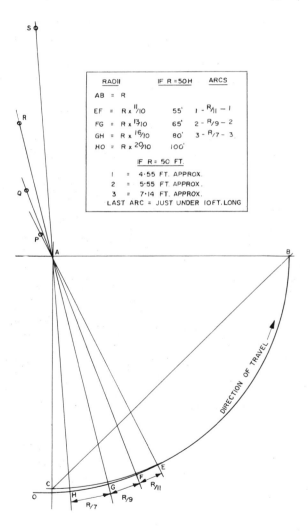

Produce EA to point P, such that PE equals $R \times \frac{11}{10}$ (Radius $\times \frac{11}{10}$). Then with P as centre and radius $R \times \frac{11}{10}$ draw arc EF to a length of $\frac{R}{11}$.

Now draw FAQ such that QF equals $R \times \frac{13}{10}$ and draw arc FG with radius QF to a length of $\frac{R}{9}$.

Again, draw GAR such that RG equals $R \times \frac{16}{10}$ and draw arc GH with a length of $\frac{R}{7}$.

Finally, draw HAS such that SH equals $R \times \frac{20}{10}$ and draw arc HO.

It is not necessary to know the length of this last arc HO, as this is only to complete the curve, the curved track joining up to the straight track at O. Thus the final transition curve is O-H-G-F-E.

CHAPTER TWELVE

Passenger Cars

PERHAPS IT IS NOT surprising that much less attention is given to the design of the rolling stock for use on the passenger-carrying railway. The builder is generally so keen to try out his new locomotive that he has to make a special effort of will to even finish the tender, let alone any rolling stock. But if the railway as a whole is to be satisfactory, and in fact safe, the passenger cars must be properly designed and soundly constructed.

It is all very well for the owner of a small railway in the back garden to run up and down his track seated on some four-wheeled crude contrivance, but if he wishes to drive his locomotive in public or on a club or society track, something better than this will naturally be expected. It should not be forgotten that the derailment of a wagon or passenger car carrying "live" passengers may even derail the whole train and the locomotive as well, with possible serious damage to the stock and even more important, casualties to the passengers.

It must also not be forgotten that on the miniature railway, the driver is fireman as well and he is also the guard; in other words, he is responsible for everything connected with the running of the locomotive and the train.

Some trucks, particularly short four-wheelers, may be quite satisfactory on straight track but uncomfortable or even dangerous on curves, especially on reverse curves; underhanging brake gear or other equipment which might catch in sleepers or tie rods can also be a source of trouble.

Generally speaking, bogie passenger cars are to be preferred for the carrying of "live" passengers, though a well-made four-wheeler of not too short a wheelbase is usually quite satisfactory to carry the driver only. The advantages of the bogie vehicle are the much greater flexibility on curves, the smoother and easier running on track which may be anything but dead true and level, and finally the use of bogies allows the body of the car to be built with a "well", so as to lower the centre of gravity of the car and its passengers. Apart from this, a bogie well wagon can be made very similar to the full-size vehicle and thus makes an attractive addition to the railway.

Derailments
Derailments WILL happen, even on the most efficiently conducted railway, but certail precautions can be taken to lessen the possibility of damage to either passengers or rolling stock. One useful precaution, applicable to both

ground level and raised tracks, is to fit each end of the passenger cars with a special deep buffer beam, the full width of the vehicle, and arranged to clear the running rails by about $\frac{3}{16}$ in. Thus if the vehicle should be derailed, the bottom edge of these deep buffer beams will engage the rails and slide along upon them, until the train can be brought to a halt. As the passenger car cannot, using these buffer beams, drop more than $\frac{3}{16}$ in., the chances of an accident are greatly reduced. On some vehicles belonging to the author, these deep buffer beams are aluminium castings, the lower edge being machined smooth and with a slight "lead" or taper at front and back edges. They have proved most effective in service.

It is most important to provide some form of valance or fender along each side of the passenger car, and these should include foot-boards, both valances and footboards being made the full length of the vehicle. While the more cautious adult passenger may feel that such refinements are unnecessary, and additional weight for the locomotive to haul, they are certainly desireable when youngsters are being carried. The danger with continuous footboards is that passengers are inclined to put one foot on one side of the vehicle while mounting or alighting from the passenger car, with the result that the car is immediately upset. However a most useful fitting is a steel bracket or stirrup, bolted to the inside of the valance on each side of the car, which engages (though it does not normally touch) a continuous steel tube (such as conduit tubing) running right round the track just below sleeper level, as shown in Fig. 34. A system similar to this has been in use on the Beech Hurst track (Sussex) for some time, and has proved most effective.

Brakes

It is most important that the driver's vehicle should have an efficient braking system and all wheels of this item should be braked. When the locomotive is hauling two or more car loads of passengers, it is asking a lot for the brakes on the driver's own vehicle to provide sufficient brake power to pull up the whole train. This is, incidentally, another reason for adopting the bogie arrangement, even for the driver's car, as there are then eight wheels that can be braked.

In some societies, drivers have even had their passenger cars equipped with a proper vacuum brake or air brake system; though considerably more work, such systems can prove most effective. On the larger gauges, $7\frac{1}{4}$ in. and upwards, some form of continuous brake becomes essential.

Although most passenger cars seen on miniature railways appear to have the conventional type of brake blocks acting directly on the treads of the wheels, as in full-size practice, there is no reason at all why other methods should not be adopted, such as a form of band brake operating on drums fitted to the axles. Another sound arrangement is to use a type of disc brake, similar to those used in the modern motor car, and the brake pads may be applied to each side of the disc either by a hydraulic system or a manual one. Where disc or inboard drum brakes are used, it is important to remember

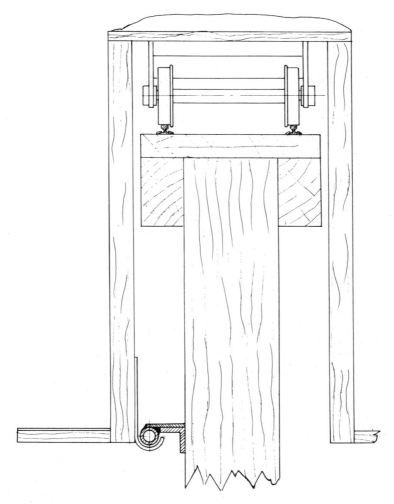

Fig. 34. Safety stirrup and tube for passenger cars. The tube may be conduit tubing welded to the brackets.

that the wheels must be a good press fit on their axles, and brake discs must be machined true, to give a smooth retardation.

Another point worthy of attention is the brake control lever itself; there has never seemed to have been any attempt at standardisation over its position or direction of operation. The author well remembers driving on a "strange" vehicle and in trying to pull up the train, pulling vainly on the lever, only to discover, in the nick of time before a collision, that the lever had to be pushed rather than pulled, to apply the brakes!

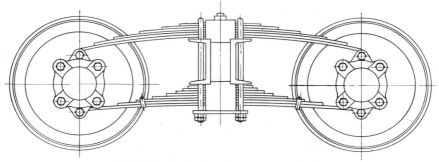

Fig. 35. Springing for a passenger car bogie.

It is suggested that all brake levers should be arranged so that the lever has to be pulled to apply the brakes, as with the hand brake on a motor car; the right-hand position also seems logical for the average driver.

If the normal type of brake blocks operating on the wheels are adopted, they should be made of cast iron, but this should be a soft grey iron, as if of too hard a grade, frequent use may wear the treads of the wheels unduly. It is clearly desirable to allow the wear to take place on the brake block, rather than on the wheel. Disc or band brakes may be lined with proper brake lining material as used on motor cars.

All the parts of the brake gear fitted to passenger cars, including cross-beams, pull rods, pins and so forth, should be of very substantial construction; all nuts should either be fitted with lock nuts or split pins, or some form of anti-vibration nut used to prevent any possibility of parts coming adrift in service.

The above remarks on brakes apply principally to the $2\frac{1}{2}$ in. to 5 in. gauge railways, but not necessarily to $7\frac{1}{4}$ in. gauge or larger. On the larger gauges, the locomotive itself becomes relatively much heavier compared with the weight of the train, so that practical braking can be applied to the locomotive in addition to that provided for the rolling stock. The larger locomotives in fact are generally fitted with a fairly powerful steam brake and in addition vacuum or air brakes may be provided, which of course will be used to operate the brakes on the whole of the train. Even on the very largest gauges such as 15 in., the brakes on the locomotive must never be expected to pull up a whole train, as the major braking effort is always applied to the passenger cars rather than to the locomotive.

Wheels

It is generally desirable to make the wheels fitted to passenger cars for the miniature railway a little heavier than the true scale equivalent, though this must be qualified by saying that the "back-to-back" measurement should be kept to the same figure as that used on the locomotives, otherwise trouble will arise when passing through points and crossings.

Sometimes one sees passenger cars fitted with very small diameter wheels,

This picture shows the very fine traverser belonging to the Birmingham S.M.E. The traverser runs on rails at right angles to the track and its construction avoids having to make a break in the main line. (Photograph—J. Balleny.)

Building the North London extension. A view looking towards the new bottom curve; the left-hand line shows sleepers already screeded awaiting the track. On the right is the 'contractor's' line for delivery of materials to site.

The brazed joints of the rails are done in pairs held temporarily by clips. Five 16 ft. lengths of rail are joined before being laid in the sleepers permanently. After laying, the long lengths are themselves brazed. (Photograph—Dave Chisnall.)

Further work on the North London extension: laying screed between the shuttering. Left to right—Bill Thrale, Dave Chisnall and Peter Roake. (Photograph—G. M. Cashmore.)

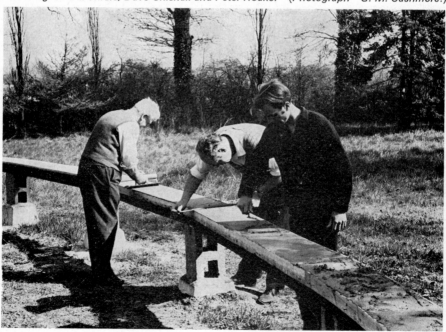

A view of the loco-
motive sidings at
the Illshaw Heath
track of the Bir-
mingham Society.

A fine stretch of
straight track on
the new Bourne-
mouth layout, taken
during construc-
tion.

Another view of the Birmingham Society's traverser.

North London Society: this picture shows the traverser in position over the main line. The traverser runs on rails laid at right angles to the track. The bar beneath the traverser operates the somersault signal. (Photograph—G. M. Cashmore.)

Part of the track of the Sussex Miniature Locomotive Society at Beech Hurst; the picture was taken during construction.

A ground level 3½ in. gauge railway under construction by Mr. F. Grosse-Holtfort, in Germany.

A ground-level 7¼ in. gauge track at New Malden. The locomotive is Mr. G. C. Smith's Southern Railway 2–6–0'

An early photograph showing the S.M.L.S. track at Beech Hurst, under construction.

A view of the new Bournemouth track, showing the site for the station. (Photograph by the author.)

This picture was taken during the construction of the new track of the Urmston Model Engineering Society.

A view of a junction on the 7¼ in. gauge Derwent Valley Railway, a ground-level line near Newcastle. (Photograph—Ken Swan.)

but this is a mistake as the larger diameter the wheels, within reason, the less will irregularities in the track be noticed. On the other hand, if the wheels are made too large in diameter, the passenger car will come out too high above the rails (unless well wagons are adopted) so that, like most things, wheel diameter must be a compromise. As a rough guide, passenger car wheels may be made the scale equivalent of 3 ft. 6 in. Thus on 5 in. gauge, the wheels would be 3¾ in. diameter approximately.

It is important that the wheel flanges of passenger car wheels are well radiused into the treads, and the treads should be tapered rather than parallel. A taper of 1 in 20 can be recommended.

Passenger car wheels are generally quite satisfactory if cast in iron, though the iron used may be somewhat harder than that generally found in model engineering work, as the much out-of-scale load of the passengers causes heavier wear on the wheel treads and flanges than is encountered on the locomotive itself. Axles should be substantial and made of mild steel, with the wheels a press fit on them, but pinning or keying of the wheels to the axles is not necessary. On tracks where the curves are of small radii, it is not a bad plan to mount the wheels on double-row ball bearings or roller bearings, the inner races of which are rigid on the axle, so that the wheels can revolve independently of one another.

Axle bearings

There is no doubt that ball or roller bearings are superior for vehicles carrying "live" passengers, owing to the greatly out-of-scale loads applied to them. If the vehicle is a four-wheeler which may have to carry two persons,

Fig. 36. An equalising passenger car bogie.

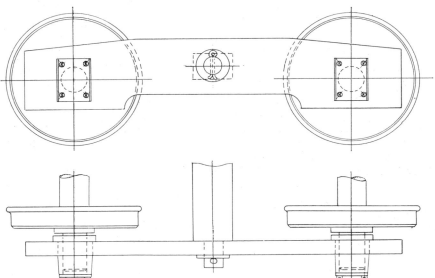

roller bearings should be used. Other types of vehicles are quite satisfactory fitted with twin self-aligning ball-races, though heavy single row bearings may be used.

Springing

All passenger cars should be fitted with some form of springing, which must be designed with due regard to the maximum load which is likely to be carried. There are many forms of springing, and some methods are shown in Fig. 35. Too much up and down movement should be avoided, owing to the danger of rolling on curves; the springs should be well up to their task, so that the vehicles do not "bottom".

If the passenger cars are of the bogie type, springing is not quite so important, as the bogies may be of the "equalising" variety, as in Fig. 36. Equalising bogies are generally very smooth running, even over quite rough track, but the pivoting of the side frames of such bogies must be of very substantial construction, otherwise the bogies will not have a long life. Bogies with single coil compression springs arranged vertically immediately above the axlebox have proved very satisfactory in service, while proper laminated springs make a first-class job for those who are prepared to spend plenty of time on the job. Other good bogie designs worth considering are those of the standard railway "diamond frame" type and the variety used by the ex-Great Western Railway for their bogie freight wagons.

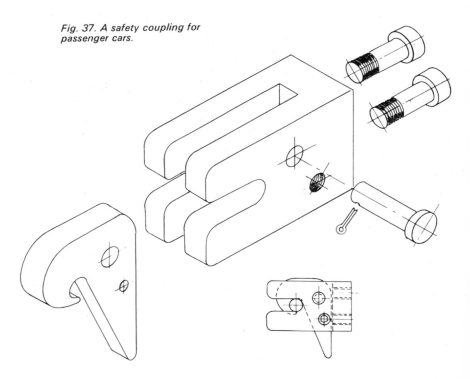

Fig. 37. A safety coupling for passenger cars.

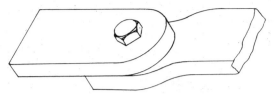

Fig. 38. A simple coupling for use between passenger cars.

Couplings

A good coupling system for passenger cars is most important. Reliance should not be placed on scale three-link couplings as used on full-size "non-fitted" wagons. A three-link coupling may appear quite reliable whilst the locomotive is pulling, but on the "over-run", or when the train is running backwards, the links of this type of coupling slacken, and may easily jump off the coupling hook.

It is not a bad scheme to provide two types of coupling for the rear of the locomotive, one being a scale model screw type coupling and the other a much more substantial and simple design which can be inserted into the rear drag beam of the engine or tender when the locomotive is required for passenger hauling service.

Where locomotives are carrying members of the general public, such as on Club tracks, the operating authorities are strongly recommended to insist on a thoroughly sound form of coupling, both between the engine and the driver's car and between each vehicle in the train. Where the coupling between the locomotive and the driving car must be of the conventional three-link type, an additional safety chain should be insisted upon.

For the couplings between the passenger cars themselves, either a proper safety coupling hook, as shown in Fig. 37 may be used, or simple steel plates, bolted and locknutted, may be adopted, as in Fig. 38.

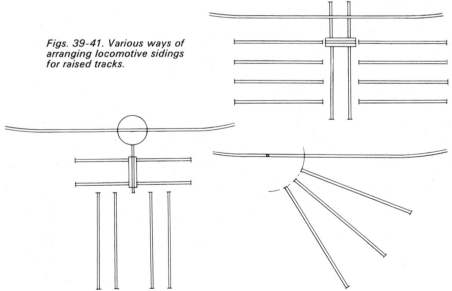

Figs. 39-41. Various ways of arranging locomotive sidings for raised tracks.

CHAPTER THIRTEEN

Signalling for Passenger-Carrying Railways

WHILE SIGNALLING ON the small gauge scenic model railway adds greatly to realism, signals on the passenger-carrying railway have a most important function to perform. Reliability is therefore most important.

Two factors must be taken into account when planning a signalling system. The first is that on a continuous line, there must be one more section than the maximum number of trains running at any time, if the trains are to run without having to stop at every signal. i.e. if there are six signals, five trains will be the maximum. The second factor is the position of the signals and their design.

A two-aspect colour light signal (red and green), or a single arm semaphore signal, must be positioned so that the driver can see it from a sufficient distance to enable him to pull up at the signal without difficulty.

A three-aspect colour light signal (red, yellow and green), or a two-arm semaphore signal (home and distant) can be placed in almost any position, as the "yellow" or "distant" will give warning to the driver that he will probably have to stop at the next "home" signal and therefore should be travelling at a slow speed and will need only about 6 ft. in which to stop.

It is proposed to refer only to colour light signals in the explanations and circuit diagrams which follow, but the solenoids or relays for operating semaphore signals can easily be substituted for the colour lights. When using semaphore signals for running in darkness, a small paraffin lamp or an electric bulb should be mounted on a bracket on the post so that the light will be seen through the spectacle to show whether the arm is "on" or "off".

For any circuit using the train on the track to operate the signalling system, the type of track must be taken into account. Track which uses tie-rods and spacers to hold the rails to the correct gauge, will require a track contact of some kind, as the rails are electrically connected together by the ties. Track which uses wooden sleepers and rail with chairs will operate the signals by the loop system, as the rails will be insulated from each other and can be electrically connected together by the wheels and axles of the train.

Another point to consider is the wiring to the signals, because if the current is high, there will be too great a voltage drop. It is always advisable to use the highest voltage possible, as this will keep the current down, the highest voltage for safety from shocks on the track being about 50 volts.

For manual circuits, alternating current from a transformer can be used, but for relay circuits, direct current from a rectifier or battery must be used. When the voltage of the supply has been decided, the current can be worked out by dividing the wattage of the lamp by the voltage, this will give the amperage. e.g.—an 18 watt lamp on a 12 volt supply will consume $1\frac{1}{2}$ amps, while a 20 watt lamp with a 50 volt supply will consume 0.4 amps.

The type of gauge of wire can now be decided by consulting the appropriate wire tables or obtaining the advice of the suppliers.

Manual signalling

For semaphore signals, a small frame with a light Bowden inner cable running through guides and around small pulleys is the least complicated system. If a signal arm is used, this will only require a single lever; if two arm signals are used, one lever will be required for the home arm and one for the distant.

A form of interlocking will also be required, so that when a home signal is "on", the distant signal applying to it is also "on". On a ground-level track with points and crossings, interlocking with the signals and points is necessary.

For all electrical circuits, whether manual or automatic, the battery polarity will be as in Fig. 44, although the voltage will only be shown when any values are important. Fig. 45 shows the position of colour-light signals on a simple continuous track. For two-aspect colour-light signals, single pole, double throw (SPDT) switches will be required, and for three-aspect signals, double pole, double throw (DPDT) switches will be needed.

The single pole, double throw switch, Fig. 46 has a centre tag which is connected to one or other of the two outer tags, depending on which way the switch is thrown, and it is wired as shown in Fig. 47, with the circuit as shown in Fig. 48.

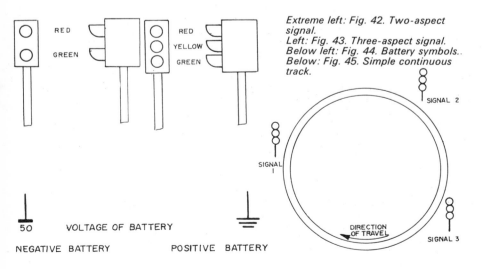

RED
GREEN

RED
YELLOW
GREEN

Extreme left: Fig. 42. Two-aspect signal.
Left: Fig. 43. Three-aspect signal.
Below left: Fig. 44. Battery symbols.
Below: Fig. 45. Simple continuous track.

SIGNAL 2

SIGNAL 1

50   VOLTAGE OF BATTERY

NEGATIVE BATTERY   POSITIVE BATTERY

DIRECTION OF TRAVEL

SIGNAL 3

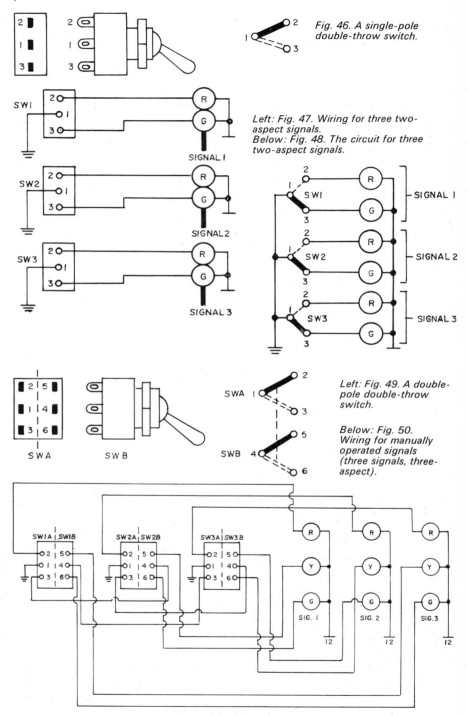

Fig. 46. A single-pole double-throw switch.

Left: Fig. 47. Wiring for three two-aspect signals.
Below: Fig. 48. The circuit for three two-aspect signals.

Left: Fig. 49. A double-pole double-throw switch.

Below: Fig. 50. Wiring for manually operated signals (three signals, three-aspect).

The double pole, double throw switch, Fig. 49 is really two single pole double throw switches mounted side-by-side in one moulding, both being operated by one toggle, and for circuitry purposes they are treated as separate switches designated A and B. (Figs. 50 and 51).

If more than three signals are required, this involves only one switch per signal extra, and for the two-aspect signal, it is only necessary to connect tag 1 to the battery "positive", tag 2 to the red lamp and tag 3 to the green lamp. For the three-aspect signal, tag 1 will be connected to the "positive", tag 2 to the red lamp, tag 3 to tag 4 of the next switch, tag 4 being connected to tag 3 of the previous switch, tag 5 to the yellow lamp of the previous signal and tag 6 to the green lamp of the previous signal.

Automatic signalling

For automatic signalling, relays replace signals. Relays are basically electrically-operated switches, and to replace a SPDT switch, a relay with one set of change-over contacts would be used. To replace a DPDT switch, a relay with two sets of change-over contacts will be used. In Fig. 52 a sectional view of a Post Office type relay is shown. a. is the winding around the pole piece b. c is the knife-edge pivot on which the armature d mounts. e, f and g are the three contacts of a "change-over" set. h is the operating pin and j is the residual stud. The items k are the insulating separators between the contacts. l are the screws which hold the contact assembly to the yoke m. n is a slotted nut which fastens the pole piece to the yoke.

The relay is mounted on a panel or bar with two screws into tapped holes p in the yoke, through two insulated bushes q, and the relay yoke is insulated from the panel by a piece of bakelite t. The two tags s are for connecting the wiring to the winding.

The working of a relay is as follows :– The battery is connected across the winding a. via tags s. and the current flowing will magnetise the pole piece b. which will attract the armature d. pivoted on the knife-edge c. (The residual stud j. is to stop the armature sticking to the pole-piece if there is any residual magnetism left when the current in the winding is switched off)

When the armature moves across to the pole-piece, the other end will lift and raise the contact f. from the contact e, and make on contact g. by moving the operating pin h. upwards. When the current is switched off, the armature moves away from the pole-piece, thus lowering the pin h., and contact f. leaves contact g. and makes on contact e. As will now be seen, this is exactly the same effect as operating a single-pole double-throw switch. The operating pin h. passes through a hole in contact e., and although fastened to it, it is insulated from contact f. (see section Fig. 53).

By lengthening the operating pin, more sets of contacts may be mounted on top of each other, so that they are all operated at the same time. There is a second pin on the other side of the armature, which will operate a second stack of contacts,—see Fig. 54 for front elevation of the relay.

When numbering the contacts of a relay, the numbering starts from the yoke, one side starting at 1 and the other side at 21, as in Fig. 54. For auto-matic signalling circuitry, four types of contacts are used, as shown in Fig. 55. A. is a pair of "make" contacts, the operating pin raises contact e. and makes it to contact f. B is a pair of "break" contacts, the operating pin raises contact f. and breaks it from contact e. C is a set of change-over contacts and as already described, the operating pin raises contact f. breaks it from contact e. and makes it to contact g. D is a set of "K" contacts; change-over contacts break before making, and K contacts make before breaking. The operating pin raises contact f. which makes to contact g. and then breaks contact g. from contact e. With all four sets of contacts, the circuit is shown.

When following the circuitry describing the systems in the following text, Fig. 56 will help. "A" shows a relay XX with a winding of 1000 ohms and four sets of contacts. "B" is the first set of contacts (K). "C" is the second set of contacts (make). "D" is the third set of contacts (change-over) and "E" is the fourth set of contacts (break).

Although manual circuits may seem to be simpler than automatic circuits, manual signalling has the disadvantage that someone must be at the controls whenever there are two or more trains on the track.

The first automatic signalling circuit (Fig. 59) is a three-aspect one operated by relays, and if compared with Fig. 51 the similarity of circuits using switches and those using relays will be seen. It is designed for use on the loop system and is for 50 volt working. If the same circuit was used for 24 volts, 400 ohm relays would be used, and for 12 volts, 150 ohm relays.

As will be seen in Fig. 57, a gap is left in one rail about 4 ft. past the signal; all other rail joints must be connected together by a length of wire of ample thickness and with sound joints, Fig. 58, to complete the electrical connection. The circuit works as follows :—

As drawn, all signals will be at green. A train is placed on the track between signals 1 and 2 and connects to two rails together through the axles and wheels of the train. Relay 1A operates, changing contact 2 of set 1A1 over from contact 1 to contact 3, extinguishes the green and lights the red of signal 1; at the same time, contact 22 of contact set 1A2 changes over from contact 21 to contact 23, extinguishes the green and lights the yellow on signal 3.

When the first wheels of the train cross the gap past signal 2, relay 2A will operate the contact set 2A1 will extinguish the green and light the red on signal 2; contact set 2A2 will change over to prepare signal 1 for yellow.

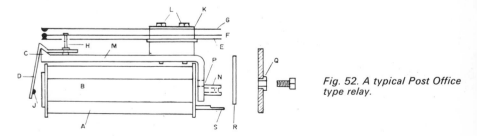

Fig. 52. A typical Post Office type relay.

Some fine bogie passenger cars seen on the 7¼ in. gauge Hilton Valley Railway.

Another view on the Hilton Valley line, showing articulated open passenger cars.

A view on the 7¼ in. gauge ground-level line of the Brighouse Society, showing 0–6–0 tank locomotive with locomotive coal wagon adapted as a driver's seat.

Some fine goods rolling stock on the 7¼ in. gauge Derwent Valley Railway.   Note the working water crane.   (Photograph—Ken Swan.)

Two four-wheel passenger cars on the permanent outdoor line of Mr. Wilkinson of Kilmacanogue, Ireland.

A 5 in. gauge "Springbok" 4–6–0 locomotive to the author's design, built by E. C. Dearman of Hazelbrook, New South Wales. Note construction of turntable. (Photograph—E. C. Dearman.)

A view on the 7¼ in. gauge Hilton Valley Railway, showing a fine covered top bogie car.

Mr. G. C. Smith's Southern Railway 2–6–0 locomotive on the New Malden $7\frac{1}{4}$ in. gauge ground-level line.

This picture shows the construction of the traverser built by the North London Society of Model Engineers. (Photograph—G. M. Cashmore.)

Another view on the Brighouse 7¼ in. gauge railway, showing passenger cars and track construction.

The water tower alongside the track of the Birmingham Society, at Illshaw Heath.

The largest standard gauge used by miniature railways is 15 in. Here is the Pacific "Green Goddess" on the Romney, Hythe and Dymchurch railway. (Photograph by the author.)

A heavy load on Lord Gretton's miniature railway at Stapleford Park. (Photograph courtesy Thames Television.)

Building a bridge for the railway to pass over a cutting at Lord Gretton's line at Stapleford Park. (Photograph courtesy Ian Allan Ltd.)

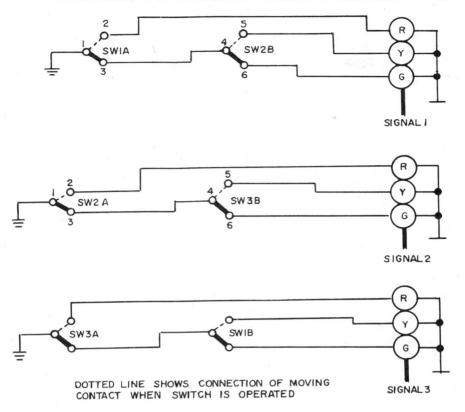

DOTTED LINE SHOWS CONNECTION OF MOVING
CONTACT WHEN SWITCH IS OPERATED

Fig. 51. The circuit for manually operated signals: three signals, three-aspect.

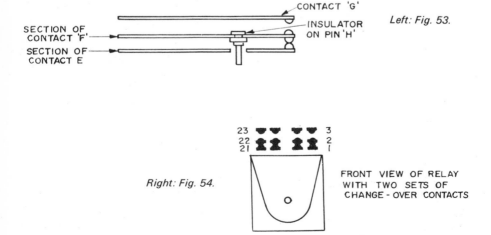

Left: Fig. 53.

Right: Fig. 54.

FRONT VIEW OF RELAY
WITH TWO SETS OF
CHANGE-OVER CONTACTS

(relay 1A is still operated by the remainder of the wheels of the train) When the whole train has passed the gap, relay 1A will fall away, contact set 1A1 will restore, changing signal 1 from red to yellow and contact set 1A2 will restore, changing signal 3 from yellow to green. When the train passes the next gap, signal 3 will change from green to red, signal 2 from red to yellow, and signal 1 from yellow to green.

As with the manual circuits, every signal added will require a relay with contact set 1 controlling the red and contact set 2 controlling the yellow and green of the previous signal.

It was mentioned previously that for automatic signalling on a track with the two rails connected together with rods and spacers, a track contact must be used. Fig. 60 shows a very simple form of track contact comprising a 6 in. length of 24 swg hard brass separated from the track by a $\frac{3}{16}$ in. thick piece of bakelite; a piece of bakelite about $\frac{1}{32}$ in. thick and about 7 in. long is fixed to the track. The end of the brass strip that protrudes beyond the thicker insulator is bent inwards so that the flanges of the wheels will "make" to it

A microswitch is shown in Fig. 61 which is operated by the weight of the train on the track. The track must be capable of being depressed about $\frac{3}{32}$ in. by the weight of the train as it passes over it, so that the switch is operated.

The circuit shown in Fig. 62 is for automatic working, using a track contact or microswitch, and operates as follows :–

The track contact or microswitch would be positioned about 4 ft. past the signal (in the same position as the gap for the loop system, Fig. 57). As the first wheels of the train pass through track contact 1, positive battery will be connected to relay 1A via the track contact and contacts 4 and 6 of contact set 1A3. Relay A1 will operate and contact 5 of contact set 1A3 will make to contact 6 and then break from contact 4, replacing the positive battery from

Fig. 59. The circuit for three three-aspect signals, operating on the loop system.

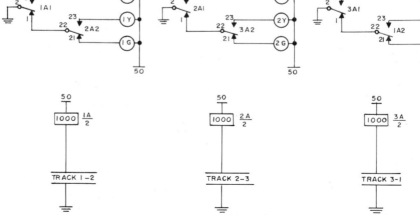

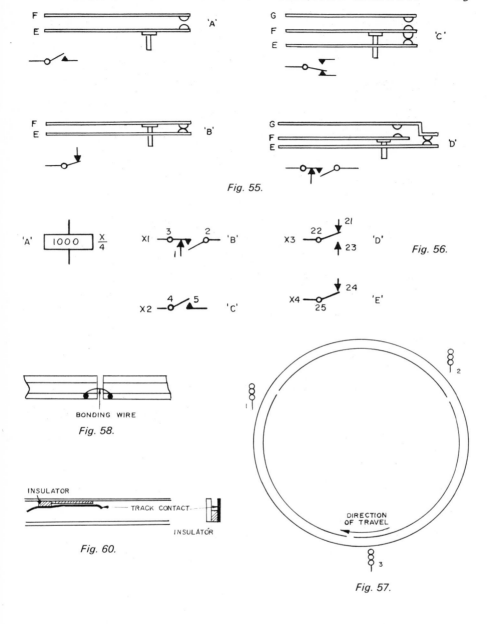

Fig. 55.

Fig. 56.

Fig. 58.

BONDING WIRE

Fig. 60.

INSULATOR
TRACK CONTACT
INSULATOR

DIRECTION
OF TRAVEL

Fig. 57.

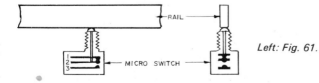

RAIL

MICRO SWITCH

Left: Fig. 61.

the track contact with the positive battery via contacts 24 and 25 of 2A4 and contacts 5 and 6 of 1A3.

Sets 1A1 and 1A2 change the signals as in the previous description (loop system). When the train wheels pass through track contact 2, relay 2A will operate through contact set 2A3 and keep operated with positive battery through 3A4 and 2A3. Contact set 2A4 will break and release relay 1A.

As can now be seen, the only difference between the loop system and the track contact system is that in the loop system the relay is held by the wheels and axles of the train completing the circuit, whereas with the track contact system the relay is held through a contact of the relay associated with the next signal.

When an automatic signalling system is used, a "track mimic panel" not only adds interest, but serves a useful purpose. The mimic should be a miniature drawing of the track, with the signals shown in their correct positions. Fig. 63 shows a mimic of the track shown in Fig. 57. The signal repeater lamps are connected to the same relay contacts as the signals and the train-on-track lamps should be white or clear and connected to the red of the miniature signal. If a signal should be reported as faulty, a glance at the mimic will tell immediately whether the fault is in the equipment or between the equipment and the signal.

Automatic Circuitry

For operating semaphore signals by automatic circuitry, a typical solenoid as shown in Fig. 64 is used. "A" is a length of brass treblet tube with a

Fig. 62. The circuit for three three-aspect signals operating on the track contact system.

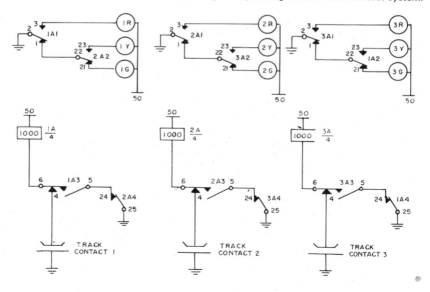

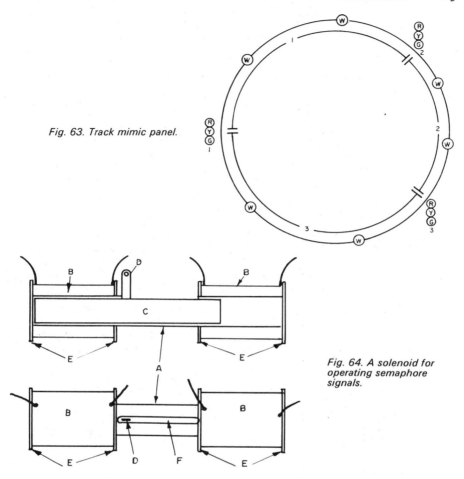

Fig. 63. Track mimic panel.

Fig. 64. A solenoid for operating semaphore signals.

winding at each end "B", the wire being held in place by bakelite formers "E". "C" is a piece of mild steel which is turned an easy sliding fit in the tube "A". "D" is the pin to operate the signal, protruding through slot "F" in the tube "A".

The operation is as follows:– With "C" in the position shown, the battery is connected to the left-hand coil, and as long as the battery remains connected, the magnetic field will hold the mild steel rod "C" over to the left-hand side. When the battery is disconnected from the left-hand coil and connected to the right-hand coil, the mild steel rod "C" will move over to the right-hand side, taking the actuating pin "D" with it. Therefore if the battery connected by the relay to the green lamp is connected to one coil, and the battery to the red lamp is connected to the other coil, the solenoid can be made to operate the semaphore arm.

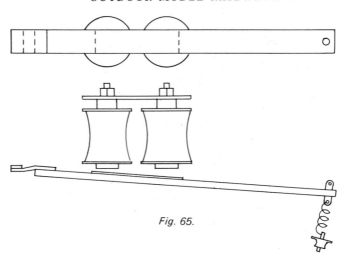

Fig. 65.

Another method is shown in Fig. 65 which uses a modified electric bell. Here, the battery is connected across the two coils so that the extended arm pulls against the spring and pulls the signal "off". When the battery is disconnected, the spring pulls the signal "on", which means that the device will "fail safe", which in some ways is to be preferred. In this case, the battery for the green lamp is connected to the "home" arm, and the battery for the "yellow" would be connected to the "distant" arm.

STANDARD DIMENSIONS

Table a. WHEELS

	A	B	D	E	P	R
0-Gauge (Coarse) (32.0)	5.00	3.50	1.50	1.50	0.50	0.50
0F-Gauge (Fine) (32.0)	3.75	2.75	1.25	1.00	0.50	0.50
1-Gauge (44·45)	6.00	4.50	2.00	1.50	0.50	0.50
1F-Gauge (Fine) (45.0)	5.00	4.00	2.00	1.00	0.50	0.50

LIMITS

Column A: +.005, −0 and 1 and 1F.
Column D: −.005, +0 in all gauges.
Column E: −.005, +0 in gauges 0 and 1 and 1F.

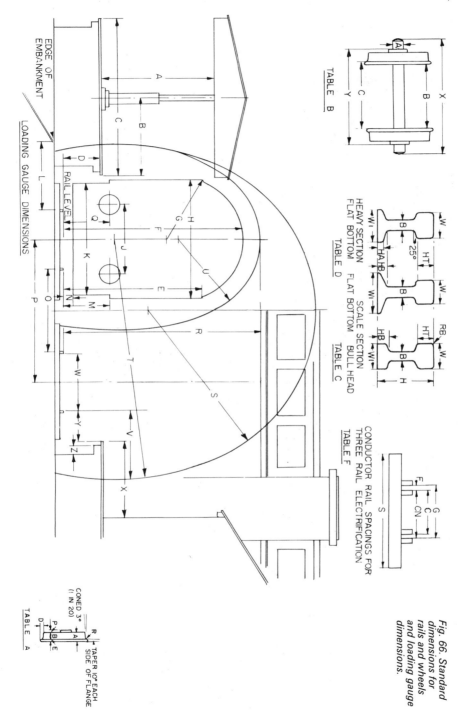

Fig. 66. Standard dimensions for rails and wheels and loading gauge dimensions.

Table b. WHEELS ON AXLES

	A	B	C	X	Y
o-Gauge (Coarse) (32.0)	2.38*	28.00	29.50	48.00	39.00
oF-Gauge (Fine) (32.0)	2.38*	29.00	30.00	45.00	37.50
1-Gauge (44.45)	3.18**	40.00	41.50	62.00	53.00
1F-Gauge (Fine) (45.0)	3.18**	42.00	43.25	62.00	53.00

$\star\ \frac{3}{32}$ inch $\star\star\ \frac{1}{8}$ inch

LIMITS
Column B and X: $+.010$ in gauges o to 1.
All above dimensions in millimetres unless otherwise stated.

Table c. BULLHEAD RAIL

	W	H	B	W¹	HT	HB	RB
oF-Gauge (Fine) (32.0)	1.50	3.50	0.80	1.50	1.16	0.76	0.20
o-Gauge (Coarse) (32.0)							
1-Gauge (44.45)	2.38	5.00	1.00	2.18	1.50	1.40	0.40
1F-Gauge (45.0)							

Table d. FLAT BOTTOM RAIL

oF-Gauge (Fine) (32.0)	1.55	3.90	0.70	3.50	1.25	1.00	—
o-Gauge (Coarse) (32.0)	2.50	5.35	1.00	3.80	2.00	1.20	—
1-Gauge (44.45)							
1F-Gauge (45.0)	2.50	5.50	1.00	5.00	1.50	1.00	—

All dimensions are millimetres unless otherwise stated.

Table e. TRACK STANDARDS

	C maxi.	F mini.	G mini.	CN mini.	S	Sleeper width
oF-Gauge (Fine) (32.0)	28.50	1.75	32.00	30.25	63.00	6.00
o-Gauge (Coarse) (32.0)	27.00	2.50	32.00	29.50	76.20	9.50
1-Gauge (44.45)	38.50	3.00	44.45	41.50	90.00	9.50
1F-Gauge (Fine) (45.00)	41.50	1.75	45.00	43.25	90.00	9.50

All dimensions are millimetres unless otherwise stated.

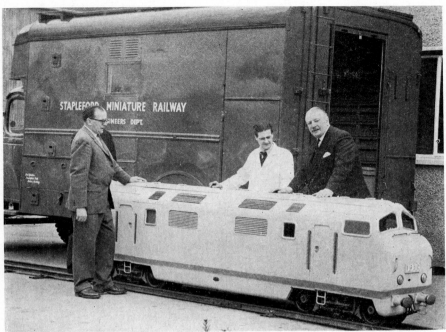

$10\frac{1}{4}$ in. gauge "diesel" locomotive on the Stapleford Miniature Railway. Right—Lord Gretton, left—the designer David Curwen.

A view on Lord Gretton's miniature railway during the filming of the television series "The Avengers". (Photograph courtesy Thames Television.)

Mr. J. Liversage's locomotive traverser.

Another picture taken during the filming of "The Avengers" at Stapleford Park. The locomotive was designed by David Curwen. (Photograph courtesy Thames Television.)

All the usual line-side features can be seen on the Stapleford Miniature Railway. This is the signal box. (Photograph courtesy Lord Gretton.)

A fine 10¼ in. gauge 4–6–4 locomotive.   (Photograph—D. H. Downie in U.S.A.)

Miniature locomotives of the larger gauges are not easy to move.   This is how Mr. J. Liversage of Herne Bay moves his 9½ in. gauge "Lord Nelson".

Facing page top.

This is one of the 15 in. gauge 4–8–2 locomotives designed by the late Henry Greenly for the Romney, Hythe and Dymchurch Railway.   (Photograph by the author.)

Facing page bottom.

Leaving Hythe station on the 15 in. gauge Romney, Hythe and Dymchurch Railway. (*Photograph by the author.*)

One of the point levers outside Hythe station on the Romney, Hythe and Dymchurch Railway. (*Photograph by the author.*)

A close-up showing the wheel and bearings of the well type turntable on the Romney, Hythe and Dymchurch Railway.

The water tower at Hythe station of the Romney, Hythe and Dymchurch Railway. (Photograph by the author.)

A view on the Goleta Valley Line in California. This is one of the finest $7\frac{1}{2}$ in. gauge railroads in the U.S.A.

Table f. CONDUCTOR RAIL SPACING FOR 3-RAIL
         ELECTRIFICATION

	Height above running rail	Distance from running rail*
o-Gauge (32.0) (Coarse and Fine)	2.00 mm.	9.00
1-Gauge (44.45)		
1F-Gauge (45.0)	3.00 mm.	14.00

*Measured from the inside face of running rail to centre of conductor rail.

SUMMARY OF GAUGES AND SCALES

Title of Gauge	Scale to the foot	Track Gauge	Equivalent Prototype Gauge in feet
Prototype	Full Size	1,435 mm.	4.71
o-Gauge (32.0)	7 mm.	32.0 mm.	4.57
oF-Gauge (Fine) (32.0)	7 mm.	32.0 mm.	4.57
1-Gauge (44.45)	10 mm.	44.45 mm.	4.44
1F-Gauge (Fine) (45.0)	10 mm.	45.0 mm.	4.50

LOADING GAUGE DIMENSIONS
All dimensions to the nearest .25 mm.

Ref. Letter	Prototype (in feet)	o Coarse 7 mm.	o Fine 7 mm.	I 10 mm.
A[1]	8.00	56.00	56.00	80.00
B[1]	6.25	43.75	43.75	62.50
C[1]	12.50	87.50	87.50	125.00
D[2]	3.0	21.00	21.00	30.00
E	10.50	73.50	73.50	105.00
F	13.50	94.50	94.50	135.00
G	5.50	38.50	38.50	55.00
H[3]	9.50	66.50	66.50	95.00
J	5.65	39.50	39.50	56.50
K	9.00	63.00	63.00	90.00
L[1]	5.30	37.00	37.00	53.00
M	3.50	24.50	24.50	35.00
N	0.75	5.25	5.25	7.50
O	6.50	53.00	45.00	65.00
P	11.15	90.00	80.00	115.00
Q	3.50	24.50	24.50	35.00
R[1]	15.00	105.00	105.00	150.00
S[4]	13.00	91.00	91.00	130.00
T[4]	19.50	136.50	136.50	195.00
U[4]	6.75	43.75	43.75	67.50
V[1]	5.33	37.25	37.25	53.25
W	4.71	32.00	32.00	45.00*
X[1]	6.00	42.00	42.00	60.00
Y**	2.40	19.00	17.50	25.00
Z[1]	1.00	7.00	7.00	10.00

NOTES

[1]   Minimum
[2]   Standard (minimum for prototype 2 ft. 9 in.)
[3]   Maximum
[4]   o Coarse Gauge, an extra 7 mm. is necessary on curves.
*   Fine Scale (44.45 mm. in Coarse Scale)
**   For straight platforms, increase on curves as necessary.

CHAPTER FOURTEEN

Public Running : Legal Liability

AT ONE TIME, the greater part of the public running carried out by small steam locomotives of 2½ in. to 5 in. gauge was done with the aid of portable tracks, usually between 50 ft. and 150 ft. in length. Generally such tracks were owned and operated by various model engineering clubs and societies. This public running is usually done at fetes or outdoor exhibitions or sports meetings, which are held either as a source of entertainment for the public, and particularly for the youngsters, or sometimes with a view to raising money for hospitals, charities and so forth.

At these events, therefore, passengers will be members of the visiting public, both adults and children, and the drivers and track staff are, therefore, undertaking a job involving certain responsibilities. These events should be in charge of responsible officials and perhaps under a senior member of the society concerned, who should preferably hold this position for a reasonable length of time, in order that experienced men may be available for the work. This gentleman may be entitled Track Superintendent.

All drivers and track staff should be prepared to carry out the instructions of the Track Superintendent, who should make himself responsible to the organisers of the meeting for the safety of the passengers and members of the public.

The first job of the Track Superintendent will be to superintend the erection of the track. He should select a suitable site which should be as firm and as level as possible. It is clearly desirable to get the track reasonably level, otherwise the passenger-carrying capacity of the railway will be impaired; a portable railway of this type may have to deal with anything between 500 and 2,000 passengers in a single day, so it is important that the locomotives should be given every chance to haul the largest possible loads.

It may be found that the track supports will have to be levelled by such materials as are available locally. Pieces of wood, bricks, concrete blocks or other materials may be used for this purpose, but it is absolutely essential that the structure be firm and safe and reasonably rigid before the first train is allowed to go into service.

If possible, the Track Superintendent should ask the organisers of the meeting to provide an enclosed space for the railway; otherwise the Society itself should arrange for some kind of fencing to prevent the public approaching too close to the line. The fencing should be of such a design that junior enthusiasts cannot get through and endanger both their own safety and that of the passengers on the trains.

Permanent Tracks

Until a few years ago, the number of permanent model railway tracks for gauges from $2\frac{1}{2}$ in. to 5 in. could be numbered on two hands, but in recent years there has been a tremendous upsurge of enthusiasm and new tracks have been built by model engineering societies all over the country, and indeed abroad. There are now societies in nearly all the large cities in England and Wales and a few in Scotland which have these fine facilities for the steam locomotive enthusiasts. The question of the safety of the line on these permanent tracks will clearly be quite a different one from that applicable to the portable track, as permanent tracks are always well provided for as regards fencing, stations, loading platforms and facilities for the locomotives.

Testing Locomotives

When the passenger-carrying track is ready for service, the Track Superintendent's next job is to satisfy himself that the engines available for service are suitable for the work to be done. It would not be very helpful to expect a small 0-4-0 "contractor's" type of engine to take turn and turn about with a big "Pacific" on heavy passenger hauling! Then there is the question of the safety of the boilers of the locomotives. No engine should be allowed to run in public unless its boiler is above suspicion and also its mechanical parts are in reasonable condition.

It would not be practicable to insist upon a boiler test for every locomotive which is about to run on the day of the event, particularly if the engine happens to belong to a visitor from another society or district. It is, therefore, normal practice for all recognised model engineering societies to arrange to test the boilers of the locomotives belonging to their own members and to give the owners certificates showing details of the tests, date when held, etc. etc., signed by responsible officers of the society. These boiler tests are normally carried out once every twelve months, and of course on the completion of any new locomotive. The boiler certificates will almost certainly be accepted by the superintendents of other tracks, when the owner of the locomotive wishes to run upon a track other than his own.

This test certificate scheme will be welcomed by all sensible drivers and owners of locomotives. No experienced driver would ever drive an engine fitted with a boiler that was in any way suspect, and no sensible locomotive owner will have any objections to his boiler being tested. After all, if he is afraid that his boiler will not pass the society's test, he should also be afraid to raise steam in it.

Under the society testing scheme, the owner is able to ensure that the boiler test is conducted in a proper manner at a suitable time and place for himself and the testing officials. Thus he does not need to allow his model to be tested by officials with whom he is not aquainted or over whom he has no control.

It cannot be too strongly emphasised that no Track Superintendent should ever take chances with an engine which has an untested boiler. Although boiler explosions are fortunately extremely rare nowadays, it must be appreciated that if a model boiler, even of a $2\frac{1}{2}$ in. gauge locomotive, should explode, it may be releasing a gallon or more of boiling water and a large quantity of steam at possibly 100 p.s.i., so that a very nasty accident could easily occur. This is not to say that model steam locomotives are in any way dangerous; in actual fact, if they are properly designed, correctly made, regularly tested, and driven in a correct and railway-like manner, the possibility of an accident is really extremely remote.

The Track Superintendent should arrange a timetable, so as to show clearly to any would-be drivers when their engines are expected to be ready, so that they can arrange to raise steam in good time to avoid delay. It is a good plan for the Superintendent to arrange that the heaviest and most powerful locomotives will be in steam when it is expected that the traffic will be at its highest peak.

Insurance

While some form of insurance is desirable to cover operations on the privately owned "back-garden" miniature railway, it is absolutely essential for public lines, whether portable or permanent. Insurance cover may be divided into three headings:—

Cover against an accident involving injury to a spectator or damage to property belonging to a spectator.

Cover against an accident involving injury to the driver of the train, or to passengers on the train, or to property belonging to driver or passengers.

Cover against an accident involving damage to the locomotive or passenger cars, to the track, or accessories appertaining to the track.

Individuals or societies running miniature railways in public must therefore see that their insurance policies cover all the above contingencies.

To take an extreme case—a boiler explosion—it is likely that the driver and a passenger or passengers would be injured, the locomotive would be badly damaged, some of the passenger cars might be slightly damaged, and if there were any spectators nearby at the time, there might be injuries to one or more spectators. This shows that all the above risks must be fully allowed for.

In the event of an accident, it may be asked—who is liable? It must be remembered that a spectator who is injured may sue either the individual who is driving the locomotive, or some other individual such as the Track Superintendent or some other responsible person in charge of operations,

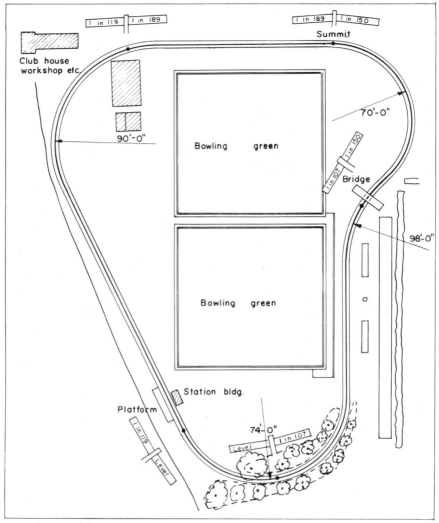

Layout of the Beech Hurst line of the Sussex Miniature Locomotive Society.

or he may sue the club or society which has organised the track meeting; or again he may sue jointly the driver and the society.

At law, the liability of a club is generally the liability of each and all of its members. It should also be remembered that the funds of a club are liable for all responsibilities of the club, and during the running of a track day, everyone directly concerned with the organisation is acting as the club's agent. Thus the club is liable for the acts of the drivers, the ticket sellers, the marshals, and the men running the locomotive department. In addition, the locomotives, though the property of individual members, are, while running at the track meeting, under the control of the club, and the club is responsible for them.

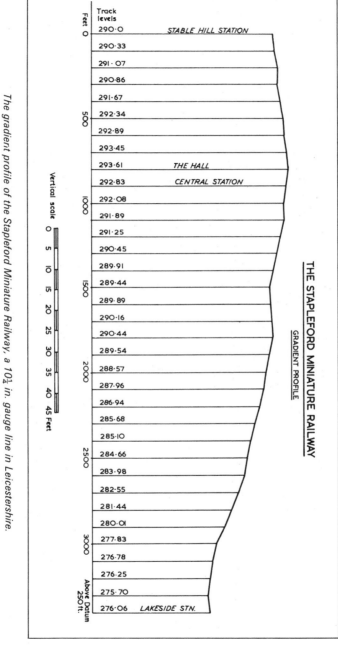

The gradient profile of the Stapleford Miniature Railway, a 10¼ in. gauge line in Leicestershire.

It should perhaps be explained that a society organising a track day cannot be held liable for an accident that nothing could have prevented—an act of God—but the society's duty is to take all proper and reasonable precautions against accidents, as has been detailed earlier in this chapter.

Another point worth noting is that club members may have rights against fellow members if such members, through negligence, cause them damage. A club member cannot sue his own club if the track collapses while he is driving his locomotive on it; but if he can prove that the collapse was due to the carelessness of another club member, he can sue that other member.

At a club track day, it may be that an accident occurs through the carelessness of the driver. Perhaps he fails to apply the brakes in time, and runs into a train ahead of him, causing damage to it, or perhaps he takes a curve too fast and has a derailment. In such a case, the driver is an agent of the club and his acts are the club's. Thus it is essential that in public functions and "open days", only competent drivers should be allowed to handle the locomotives. But even the most experienced driver can make a mistake, and the club and its funds could become liable for his negligence. It is however not certain just how far individual committee men and ordinary club members could be held liable in such a case, and it may be that a committee man who has taken no direct part in the management of the function would not be liable for the unfortunate lapse of the driver.

It is of course possible for a club to limit its liability to invited drivers and also to passengers on its trains by making a special contract with them. Such a contract can be effected by a notice clearly exhibited so that all visitors cannot fail to see it, the notice stating that they drove or rode upon the track in all respects at their own risk, and that the club did not in any way guarantee the safety of the track, locomotives or rolling stock. Of course it may be questioned whether such expedients are really in the interest of the club, and whether they would not tend to discourage use of the track. It may therefore be said that the wisest course for a club to take is to accept its liabilities and take all possible steps to prevent accidents arising.

A final point to be remembered is that, while an ordinary club is, from a legal point of view, the aggregate of its members, and an insurance policy protecting the club from liability protects its members also, this is not the case as regards a company, which is a separate legal entity. (Some clubs are limited liability companies). Care should therefore be taken in effecting insurance policies to see that the individual members, as well as the company are protected.

The reader may be somewhat surprised at the legal complications that can arise in connection with the organising of a track "open day" or public meeting. But in fact, the safety provisions necessary are really very simple, and once the club or the individual club member has become accustomed to them, they will not be found to be in any way detrimental to the enjoyment of one of the most fascinating branches of the hobby of model engineering—the operation of the miniature steam locomotive.

This photograph shows the construction of the turnouts on the Romney, Hythe and Dymchurch Railway. Note how the tie-rods are connected to the point blades. (Photograph by the author.)

An unusual bogie passenger vehicle seen on the Romney, Hythe and Dymchurch Railway. Note the "instanter" couplings and vacuum brake pipes. (Photograph by the author.)

This picture shows some of the point work outside Hythe station of the Romney, Hythe and Dymchurch Railway. A train about to leave headed by one of Greenly's "Pacifics". (Photograph by the author.)

A well type turntable on the 15 in. gauge Romney, Hythe and Dymchurch Railway. Engine sheds and workshops in background. (Photograph by the author.)

A close-up of one of the turnouts on the Romney, Hythe and Dymchurch Railway, showing point-rodding, angle cranks and guides.   (Photograph by the author.)

A fine turntable on the 7½ in. gauge Goleta Valley Line in California, U.S.A.

Top left: steel girder bridge over the River Lea, built for the former Midland Railway. Middle left: another view of the same bridge. Bottom left: lattice girder bridge built for the former Great Eastern Railway, crossing the River Lea at Walthamstow. Top right: an early plate girder bridge crossing a tributary of the River Lea near Walthamstow, built for the former Great Eastern railway. Lower right: another view of the lattice girder bridge. (Photographs by the author.)